# Setting Up a
# TROPICAL
# AQUARIUM
## SECOND EDITION

# Setting Up a
# TROPICAL AQUARIUM
## Week-by-Week
### SECOND EDITION

FIREFLY BOOKS

# A Firefly Book

Published by Firefly Books Ltd. 2015

First printing

**Publisher Cataloging-in-Publication Data (U.S.)**

Thraves, Stuart, 1970–
     Setting up a tropical aquarium : week-by-week / Stuart Thraves.
2nd edition
[208] pages : color photographs ; cm.
Includes index.
Summary: "Detailed descriptions of 50 aquarium plants and 100 popular freshwater aquarium fish are featured as they are added to the tank, rather than in separate unrelated sections" — Provided by publisher.
ISBN-13: 978-1-77085-518-2 (pbk.)
1. Aquariums. 2. Tropical fish. I. Title
639.34 dc23  SF457.3.T5738 2015

**Library and Archives Canada Cataloguing in Publication**

Thraves, Stuart, 1970–, author
     Setting up a tropical aquarium week-by-week / Stuart Thraves. -- Second edition.
Includes index.
ISBN 978-1-77085-518-2 (pbk.)
     1. Aquariums. 2. Tropical fish. I. Title.
SF457.3.T48 2015    639.34   C2015-902940-6

Published in the United States by
Firefly Books (U.S.) Inc.
P.O. Box 1338, Ellicott Station
Buffalo, New York 14205

Published in Canada by
Firefly Books Ltd.
50 Staples Avenue, Unit 1
Richmond Hill, Ontario L4B 0A7

Photography: Geoff Rogers
Design and prepress: Stuart Watkinson, Philip Clucas
Created and edited: Ideas into Print, Claydon, Suffolk
     IP6 0AB, England.
Print production: 1010 Printing, China

Printed in China

## The Author

Stuart Thraves has had a lifelong fascination with fish. This led him to study them at Sparsholt College in Hampshire, England. Thraves' interest in fish has also developed into a favorite hobby – diving – which he enjoys pursuing around the UK and in the Red Sea.

## The Consultant

Adrian Love has been keeping fish for over 30 years, an interest that has taken him from the jungles of Borneo to the African plains. He has worked in ornamental fish farms and fish culture facilities and now lectures in fish husbandry at Sparsholt College, Hampshire.

**Above:** *A freshly planted display aquarium with newly introduced fish exploring their environment. As the system matures, more fish can be added and the tank will become an underwater world.*

# INTRODUCTION

We are constantly fascinated with other worlds. Apart from outer space, the only other domain we have yet to completely explore is the underwater world. It is a world of sumptuous variety, from the swirling sun-drenched waters of a coral reef to the tranquil shadows of an Amazon stream trickling slowly beneath a canopy of heavy-leaved tropical trees. These are just two examples of many thriving habitats in which plants, fish and invertebrates live together in aquatic harmony.

Since the great age of discovery and invention in Victorian times, we have tried to bring this fascinating spectacle into our homes. The first aquariums were simple boxes with glass fronts in which temperate fish species were kept. With little appreciation of their needs, the fish soon expired and had to be replaced regularly. This approach would be totally unacceptable today with our regard for animal welfare. A greater understanding of how natural cycles work and the technology to sustain them now offers fishkeepers the exciting opportunity to create and maintain aquariums that will thrive for many years.

This book follows the sequence of setting up and running a tropical freshwater aquarium for the first twelve weeks of its life. At logical points along the timeline of practical progress there are profile sections that feature extended selections of suitable plants and fish. Throughout, the emphasis is on explaining how vital life-support systems work, including the basic science behind the processes they depend on. Unlike many hobbies, where learning can be phased and levels of difficulty matched with emerging ability, fishkeeping requires the immediate grasp of a crucial technique — how to turn a transparent box of water into an environment that will sustain life from day one and beyond. Fishkeepers are pet owners, with all the responsibilities that title entails. How you control that environment dictates whether your display will thrive or deteriorate into an unsightly mess. This book will give you a head start in the quest to be successful.

# CONTENTS

## DAY 1
**14** Building the system

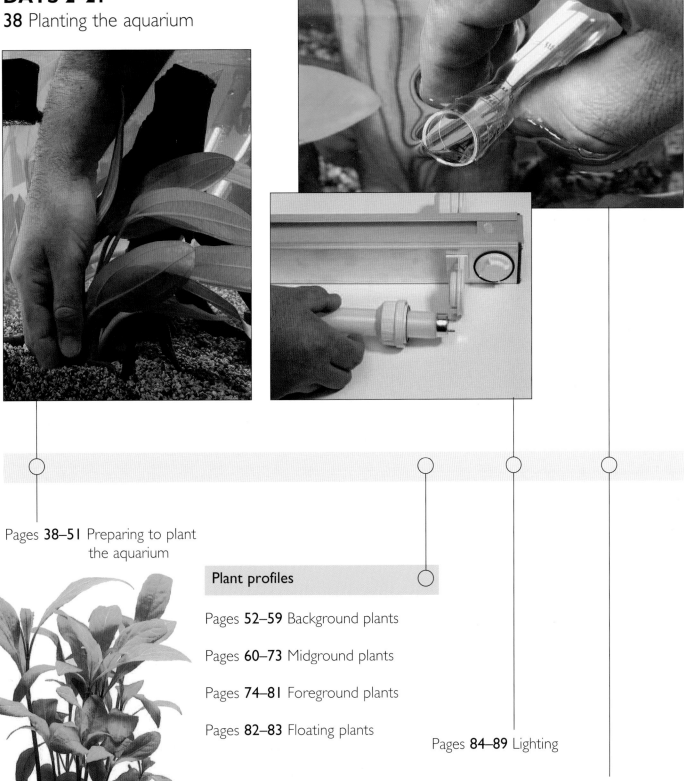

## DAYS 2–21
### 38 Planting the aquarium

# CONTENTS

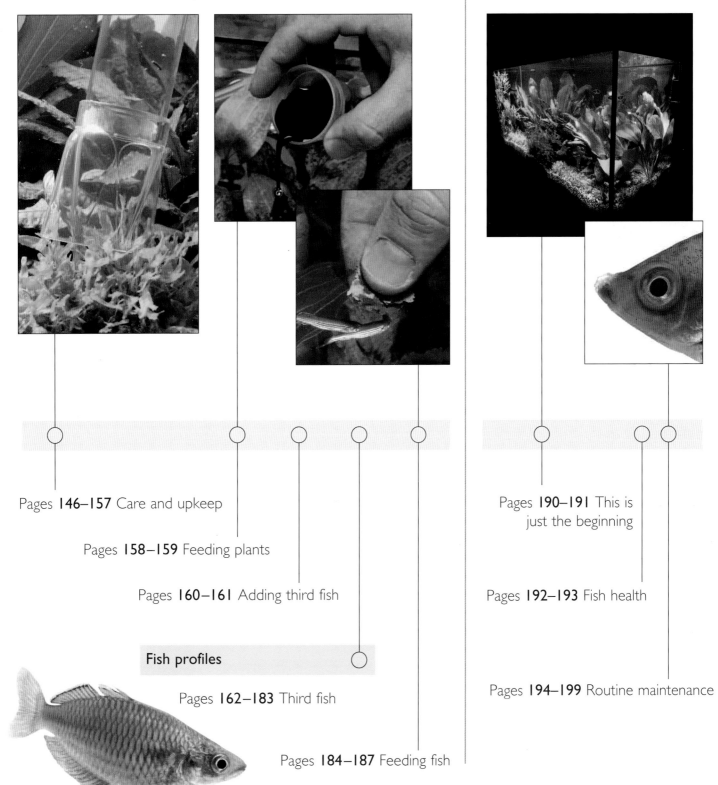

# WEEK 8
## 144 Toward a stable system

# WEEK 12
## 188 The finished display

## FIRST THOUGHTS AND DECISIONS

When you have decided to set up a tropical freshwater aquarium, your crucial first decision is where you would place it in your home. Clearly, it will dictate the size and shape of tank you can consider.

### Choosing a location

There is usually a place in every home suitable for an aquarium. Its location can have a great influence on how successful an aquarium is. It might mean changing the layout of an entire room to accommodate the aquarium in its best position. A good idea is to draw the layout of the room on paper and sketch in the likely positions of the aquarium. This could save hours of moving furniture and then finding out that everything simply will not fit!

Choose a location that will present the aquarium as a focal point in a room where people spend the most time relaxing in the evenings or at mealtimes. A favorite place for an aquarium is as a room divider, enabling the aquarium to be viewed from both sides. It can also be set into a wall to provide the classic "living picture."

Once you have chosen a suitable location, check that the tank support is strong enough. This includes checking that any pre-assembled cabinets have all the bracing pieces fitted. The aquarium featured in this book measures 90 cm (36 in) long, 38 cm (15 in) from front to back and 45 cm (18 in) high. Such an aquarium full of water will weigh about 150 kg (330 lb)! Also check that the floor can support the weight. The essential rule is that the aquarium should run across several floor joists and not along a single joist. If in doubt, consult a qualified builder for advice.

Finally, check that you can get the tank to the room in the first place. Aquariums are not flexible or available flat-packed and are generally very heavy, awkward and fragile to handle.

### Selecting a tank

When you have a suitable location in mind, choosing a tank is your next decision. There are many shapes and sizes available today, and it is a good idea to seek expert guidance from your local retailer.

### Think of the fish

The first golden rule to consider when buying an aquarium is that it must provide the correct conditions for your fish to survive. Like us, fish breathe oxygen and exhale carbon dioxide. These gases are dissolved in the water and get in and out at the surface. Therefore, any aquarium must provide a large surface area to allow sufficient exchange of gases.

This key point greatly influences the optimum design for an aquarium. Fortunately, the best design from a "life-support" point of view also looks pretty good in the living room! Since we are aiming to create a living picture that recreates an underwater scene, the most effective and compelling format is a rectangular aquarium that provides

### Siting the aquarium

*This is the ideal corner location in this room for an aquarium. The aquarium will need power to function. Electrical sockets should be nearby, but not directly underneath.*

*Fitting dimmer switches to main room lights will reduce the shock to fish of suddenly turning on bright lights.*

*Heat from radiators will affect the aquarium*

*Avoid direct sunlight, as the excess light will stimulate unsightly algae growth.*

*Do not use bookshelves because they are seldom strong enough to support a heavy aquarium. However, custom-designed shelves can be used if the loading is worked out and taken into consideration beforehand.*

*Doors opening and closing suddenly can stress fish. Avoid drafty areas because these will cause fluctuating water temperatures.*

*Avoid locating the aquarium close to loudspeakers or the TV. The fish will be stressed by the constant vibrations.*

**Right:** All tanks should have a large surface area to allow oxygen to be absorbed and carbon dioxide to leave the water. Cube-shaped aquariums provide interesting viewing aspects, along with an acceptable surface area in relation to depth.

**Above:** A rectangular aquarium is a traditional choice and the shape we have chosen to set up. This tank is 90x38x45 cm deep (36x15x18 in) and holds 150 liters (33 gallons) of water.

**Above:** Fishkeepers today have a wide choice of aquarium shapes and sizes. This curved tank on a custom-designed stand is supplied with lighting and filtration equipment included.

**Left:** Even a small well-furnished aquarium (this one is only 48 liters/ 10.5 gallons capacity) can become a fascinating focal point in any room. But bear in mind that to keep it looking its best means carrying out regular maintenance, including water changes. Is there a water source nearby or will you have to carry heavy buckets back and forth each time?

a "widescreen" landscape view. This is ideal for the fish because it offers a large surface area in relation to the volume of water in the tank.

This principle effectively rules out the tall column-style aquarium, which has a relatively small surface area. Only a few fish could be kept in this style of aquarium and would need a great deal more care than they would in a landscape format aquarium.

"Permissible" variations on a landscape theme include the bow-fronted aquarium — in a rectangular or corner shape — as well as six-sided aquariums. Also, compact cube aquariums are popular and ideal for small rooms.

## Buy as big as you can
Aim to buy the biggest aquarium you can afford and accommodate. The simple reason for this is that when keeping fish the larger the volume of water you have to play with the easier it will be to control the waste products the fish produce and hence provide a stable environment. Although there are effective filtration systems available, the larger the volume of water you provide the better it will be for your fish in the long term.

## Final checks before buying
Before you decide on the aquarium that suits your requirements, ask yourself the following questions as a mini checklist to avoid possible problems in the future. How much access to the aquarium is there once the lid is on? How easy will it be to carry out regular maintenance? If the aquarium has a built-in life-support system, is this simple to maintain? Always check the glass of the aquarium and reject any with slight chips, since these are potential weak points. Even a compact aquarium holds a great deal of water that, together with the plants, rocks, equipment and fish, will make a fine mess of your living room floor if it shatters!

## Attaching a background
Once your aquarium is set up and you are enjoying the relaxing effect of watching your fish, the last thing you want to see is cables and pipes behind the algae-speckled glass back of the tank. A background will hide all those cables and provide a more neutral backdrop to show your fish, plants and decor at their best. Dark backgrounds will reduce the appearance of algae and will also make your fish feel safer and, therefore, improve their health. Three-dimensional backgrounds can create a natural setting on which to base your style of aquascape, but bear in mind that once in place, a background is very difficult to change. In our step-by-step sequence we have not fitted a background so that we can more clearly show the practical sequence of setting up the aquarium.

## Sheet backgrounds
The simplest form of background is a plastic sheet that fits on the outside of the aquarium. These are available in many colors, variations and designs, ranging from natural planted displays and rockscapes to dramatic landscapes. If you are not sure which design is best for your tank, stick to a plain black background. This will show up the colors of your fish to their best advantage and focuses attention onto

*Above:* Odessa barbs are a shoaling species, so keep them in groups. Give them swimming space, as well as areas of dense vegetation that provide hiding places and look decorative and natural.

*Right:* Cube aquariums provide great opportunities for creative planting. In this tank, a black background has been applied to the rear panel so that the display can be viewed from three sides. The heater and filter occupy one corner.

**Above:** *Take care when choosing your background design — once in place a background is hard to remove. Natural designs or plain black often look better than more colorful designs.*

the objects you place in the tank. Sheet backgrounds can be easily attached with adhesive foam pads, but these leave gaps where drips of water can fall between the background and the tank, leaving a visible and unsightly mark. A better method is to use double-sided tape along the top and sides of the tank and roll the background out along the glass; any excess can be trimmed from the bottom and sides once the background is attached. It may take a few attempts to get the background on without any creases, but it is a job that will only need doing once.

## Attaching a background sheet

**1** *Place strips of double-sided tape along the top of the aquarium glass and vertically at each end of the glass panel.*

**2** *Overlap the strips to make sure there are no gaps. Peel away the backing layer of the tape, exposing the sticky side.*

**3** *Carefully roll out the background and try to avoid creases. Do this lightly at first so that mistakes can be easily fixed.*

**4** *Once the background is flat, secure it by pressing it firmly against the glass and then trim off any excess around the edges.*

## Molded backgrounds

For a more realistic and visually appealing background, consider using a molded background specially designed for the aquarium. There are various designs, usually with a rock-like appearance or featuring tree-root structures. A molded background will be a big factor in the overall appearance of the aquarium, and you can also grow mosses or object-rooting plants on it. Choose wisely, though;

a molded background is a permanent fixture and cannot be removed easily without stripping down the whole tank.

Molded backgrounds are available in a number of sizes, but in most cases you will need to buy a near fit and trim off any excess using a craft knife. Once cut to shape, fix the background in place with readily available aquarium silicone sealant before filling the tank.

**Above:** *Three-dimensional molded backgrounds give a more natural look.*

**Left:** *The crevices in this design are ideal for growing mosslike plants.*

**Left:** *Molded backgrounds are very buoyant and should be fixed in place with silicone sealant when the tank is dry. Only use aquarium sealant and allow at least 48 hours for it to dry.*

13

# BUILDING THE SYSTEM

Along with your choice of aquarium there is a wide range of accessories you will need to get up and running, and to maintain the tank over a longer period. It is worth thinking about these items from the start, and using a checklist to make sure you have everything on hand. Familiarising yourself with these items will help you to work out your total budget for choosing your tank, and you may even be able to get some items at a discounted price if you buy them with the aquarium. With the exception of the carbon dioxide unit, which is discussed later on, all of the items shown in the panels below are essential for your tank.

*Right: See what equipment your chosen tank contains and make a list of all the extras you need. Your retailer may even offer you a discount.*

### Items needed to start
- Filtration
- Heaterstat
- Thermometer (optional)
- Substrate
- Water testing kits
- Dechlorinator
- Bacterial starter (optional)
- Basic dry food
- Decor & plants
- Background
- Bucket
- Carbon dioxide unit (optional)

### Items needed for long-term care
- Algae cleaning pad
- Cloth or disposable towels
- Gravel cleaner
- Siphon hose
- Additional foods
- Replacement filter media(s)
- Net for debris removal
- Plant fertilizers

*Check the aquarium glass for any obvious chips or scratches. These could expand under the pressure of water.*

*Leveling the tank is the first vital step; even a slight discrepancy will be obvious once you add water to the aquarium. Use a long spirit level. If necessary, rest it on a straight wooden batten.*

The first day of the setting up process will be dominated by positioning the tank, installing the equipment and introducing the first of the hard landscaping decor into the aquarium. However, by the end of day one you will begin to have a good idea of how the display will look.

Before you start assembling the equipment you have bought from the aquarium shop, make sure you have the following tools in hand:

- A long spirit level
- Screwdriver
- Sharp scissors
- Nail or scrubbing brush
- Water jug
- A couple of old towels
- A four-way electrical extension
- A plug-in 24-hour timer
- Double-sided sticky tape for attaching the background (see page 13)
- Cable ties
- A 10-liter (2-gallon) plastic bucket

The bucket is one item that you will need for the entire life of the display, for transporting both clean and waste water. It is also the ideal place to store all your aquarium maintenance equipment. It is a good idea to choose one with clear markings so that measuring out the water capacity for your display will be easy. Alternatively, you can put your own markings on the outside.

You may also like to set aside some dry clothes in case your sleeves get wet or you are splashed during the setting up process.

## First steps

Once you have chosen your aquarium and decided where to put it, you can begin the enjoyable task of setting it up. It is vital to proceed carefully in a patient frame of mind, following the step-by-step instructions provided here. Rushing to finish the display and failing to allow the emerging aquarium to mature at certain critical stages during the first few weeks will cause problems later on and dispel the good feeling you had at the outset.

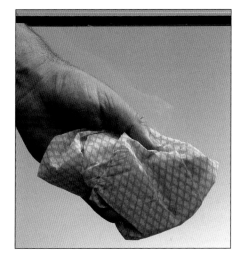

**Above:** *Wipe the inside of the glass with a clean cloth to remove dust, otherwise it will create a film on the water surface. Also clean the exterior and remove any marks left by the packaging.*

## Level and clean

When you have unpacked all the equipment and positioned the tank on the cabinet or stand, the first task is to make sure that the tank is level, both from front to back and side to side. This is crucial, not only because a "sloping" water level will look unnatural and disturbing, but also because a tank that is not level is potentially unstable. Always adjust the cabinet or stand and not the tank. Placing wedges under a glass tank full of water will create stress that may cause the glass to fracture. For the same reason, rest the tank on a plastic foam or polystyrene mat to compensate for slight irregularities in the surface of the support. (This is not necessary for stands that support the tank around the perimeter of the base.)

The next job is to wipe the inside and outside surfaces with a damp cloth. The tank may have been in the shop for a few weeks and will have a coating of dust that should be removed. Use a clean cloth — ideally a new one — that has no chemical cleaning agents on it.

## ADDING SUBSTRATE

With the bare tank level, clean and in position with a suitable background fitted, it is now ready for the components that will create and maintain our living underwater scene. Working from the bottom up, the first layer to add is the substrate, and the majority of substrates will need washing first. Placed directly in the aquarium, unwashed substrate would transform an aquarium into a cloudy maelstrom that any filtration system would have difficulty clearing. It is essential, therefore, to wash the substrate before use. Even apparently clean substrate will produce dirty water when first rinsed. To clean the substrate, simply wash it in several changes of tap water in a bucket until the water is clear. To speed up the removal of heavy dirt, use boiling water, but be sure to stir this with a large spoon or similar implement to avoid scalding your hands.

### The role of the substrate
The substrate creates a natural "bed"

within the aquarium and supports any rocks and wood that you may add as part of the decor. Some fish like digging around in it, searching for bits of food. In an aquarium without live, rooted plants the substrate just needs to please the aesthetic taste of the owner and the needs of the fish. In a planted tank, however, the substrate plays a crucial role in anchoring and nourishing the plants that will grow through it. Often, a single substrate is used over the whole aquarium, but different substrates can look equally effective. In this way "plant-substrates" can be used in areas that will be heavily planted, and open areas can be laid with the usual gravel or sand. Whatever you decide, it is vital to get the substrate right from the start as it cannot be easily changed later on. Initially, the wide range of substrates available can be confusing, but they can be grouped in terms of what they provide for the plants.

### Substrate Options

These provide all the nutrients the plants need in one product. They are available in a range of colors and granule sizes. They may seem relatively expensive but are very convenient.

### Base layers/additives
These substrates contain highly concentrated levels of nutrients that you

**Above:** *This nutrient-rich additive is ideal for heavily planted aquariums. It is designed to be laid under the main substrate and will nourish plants via the roots growing into it.*

**Below:** *These clay balls are loaded with nutrients, providing a targeted extra supply for individual plants. Simply bury them in the substrate near the roots as required.*

**Above:** *Wash the substrate thoroughly in a bucket. Do not try to clean it all at once; instead, place a small amount in the water and agitate it until the water runs clear.*

**Above:** *Pour the cleaned substrate carefully into the tank in small batches, levelling it as you work. Add a final layer to create a finished depth of about 10 cm (4 in).*

## Undergravel heater

An alternative to a traditional heater is one that lies under the gravel. They are designed to boost the ambient temperature of the water (by about 5°C/9°F) rather than keep it within a specified temperature range. They offer two advantages: first, they create tiny currents in the gravel, through which oxygen and nutrients may be distributed. Second, being hidden under the gravel, they are invisible. The alternative is to hide traditional heaters behind plants and decor, which is not always easy to do, particularly in small tanks. Because of their low capacity (often 7–15 watts), they suit cool water aquariums.

*Left:* Heating pads are designed to gently increase the water temperature in small aquariums. They can be fixed to the inside of the tank or, as here, buried under a layer of gravel.

sandwich between layers of normal gravel or sand. You do not need a lot and so they seem less expensive than complete substrates, but you do need to factor in the additional cost of the gravel or sand.

### Tablets/sticks

Again, these products are used in conjunction with normal gravel or sand. They are supplied as little packages of nutrients that slowly release food when they are buried next to the plant roots. Unlike base layers, root tabs can be added at any time so these are the best options when you have a tank with a gravel bottom but want to start growing plants in it. Some need replacing more often, or contain a narrower range of nutrients, than others so it is worth checking the label to see what you are getting.

### Sand

Sand can look stunning on the bottom of an aquarium. It is available in a range of colors, and many types of fish really enjoy sifting through it. Always use aquarium sand rather than builder's sand, which has very fine particles that will cloud the

*Left:* Pea gravel does not make a good plant substrate on its own, but can be used as a thin top layer. Experiment with combining different grades for a more interesting effect.

water. Fine sands may compact and are unsuitable as a plant substrate; but they can still be used in open areas of the aquarium, simulating a sand bank of a jungle stream. Do not place a fine layer of sand over gravel as within a few months all the sand will work its way underneath the gravel particles.

### Pea gravel

The most commonly available medium for the base of an aquarium is pea gravel, so called because of its rounded, pealike grains. This is available in a range of particle sizes, the most useful of which is 5 mm (0.2 in). This grade of pea gravel will have a fairly open structure and should not pack down too tightly over time, allowing oxygenated water to slowly circulate to all levels and prevent any area within the substrate bed from becoming stagnant and anaerobic (starved of oxygen).

If you have soft water as your main supply, the mineral content of the gravel will help to buffer the water (resist change) and provide a stable neutral to slightly alkaline pH (see page 91). If your water is relatively hard and slightly alkaline to start with and you want to create more acid conditions, perhaps to suit certain fish, you may find it difficult to lower the pH if you use pea gravel, since the mineral content in the substrate will bring it back to neutral or alkaline pH values. In this case, consider using one of the completely inert substrates, such as lime-free quartz gravel, that will not affect your water chemistry in any way.

## Quartz gravel

Quartz gravel is an inert granular material that is ideal for most aquarium setups. Colors can vary, with a dark sandy shade being the most commonly available. The grade best suited to aquarium use has a particle size of 1–3 mm (0.04– 0.12 in). This forms an excellent substrate that will allow good root penetration and growth to support a healthy plant. As with other gravel substrates, quartz gravel will need to be combined with laterite or similar nutrient material in the mid to lower levels to support plant growth.

*Lime-free gravel makes an excellent inert main substrate and is a good planting medium.*

**Above:** *Here, the substrate is a mixture of gravels and small pebbles to emulate a streambed. It is surprisingly easy to alter the texture and color of the substrate.*

**Right:** *If you choose a sandy substrate to emulate a particular natural habitat, disturb it regularly with your fingers to prevent stagnation. Clear away algae and debris with a clear siphon tube.*

**Below:** *A mixture of substrates provides a more useful planting medium than a single material.*

*Pea gravel is commonly available and cheap to buy. Mixed grades add variety and combine well with larger rocks and pebbles.*

*Red chippings add color and texture. Chippings are available in various colors. For the best effect, choose ones that match the rocks in the tank.*

*Black quartz makes a good contrast to the more usual golden-brown color.*

## Using soil in the aquarium

Although soil may appear to be the obvious choice as a plant-growing medium in an aquarium, it is much less practical than the many products that are specifically made for planted tanks. However, if you develop your skills and like the challenge of using soils as the main rooting medium, there are a few key requirements for success. First, make sure the soil you use is suitable: garden soil will contain unwanted nutrients and life that will be incompatible with being submerged, as well as potentially harmful pesticides and other debris that might rot. Furthermore, any compost with added peat can turn the water very acidic over time. The only recommended option is to use sterilized "aqua-soil" sold for use in pond plant baskets. Second, cover the soil thoroughly with gravel or sand, otherwise any slight disturbance from the fish will generate clouds of soil and spikes of nutrients in the water that will encourage fast-growing algae. Similarly, planting must be done carefully to avoid soil being exposed, and once the tank is planted it is essential that the substrate remains undisturbed. Any alterations or moving of plants will turn the water into a mud soup that will require a complete strip down of the messy aquarium and a fresh start. All that said, some people use soil in aquariums very effectively; it contains long-lasting iron and other nutrients that remove the need for subsequent fertilization, and as the organic matter of the soil is broken down the process releases carbon dioxide that the plants will use.

*Take care when using soil in the aquarium.*

# FITTING THE FILTER, HEATER AND $CO_2$ SYSTEM

A filter is one of the most essential pieces of aquarium equipment. Not surprisingly, there is a huge array of types and sizes available. Nevertheless, all filters are designed to perform the same basic tasks: to remove solid waste from the aquarium and offer a place of refuge to billions of "good" bacteria that will keep water conditions optimum. A third function is to chemically remove waste from the water with products (such as activated carbon) that absorb specific toxins.

Some aquariums have a filter built in. This is a simple and straightforward option and the filter will be the right capacity for the size of aquarium. Alternatively, you may want a style, shape or size of aquarium that requires a separate filter. In this case there are a few alternatives that differ in where

they are positioned (inside or outside the aquarium), their output, and how they are powered (with air or a pump). Essentially, filters provide so-called mechanical filtration — removal of solid waste; biological filtration — removal of dissolved waste through the use of bacteria; and chemical filtration, which is used now and then. With the most basic filters, the mechanical and biological filtration are done by the same material (called filter media), but more sophisticated filters offer more space and more opportunity to employ advanced filter media.

## The internal power filter

Our system uses a compact internal power filter that sits discreetly in the back corner of the aquarium. A submersible

water pump at the top of the unit draws water through the filter medium and circulates it back into the tank. The filter medium is a simple block of open cell plastic foam that admirably performs the twin roles of trapping solid debris from the water flow and providing a large surface area for beneficial bacteria. Many internal filters are designed to allow the filter media to be easily removed for maintenance or to be replaced.

The filter body clips into a plastic cradle fixed to the glass with suction cups. Starting with a new clean tank makes fixing suction cups easy and reliable: suction cups submerged for many months do become difficult to fix onto glass, especially dirty glass. Turn the filter in the cradle so that the return (cleaned) water flow is directed diagonally across the tank.

## An internal power filter

*Filter cradle*

*Filter foam supports the growth of beneficial bacteria.*

*Electric motor that drives an impeller, creating water movement.*

**Right:** *Insert the filter into the cradle gently, otherwise the housing could break or come away from the glass.*

**Below:** *Secure the filter cradle to the glass using the suckers supplied.*

*Separate compartment for activated carbon.*

*Activated carbon filter medium.*

## The internal filter in position

*Left:* Dirty water is drawn into the filter at the base, so be sure to position the unit well above the substrate. Once cleaned, the water returns to the tank via the nozzle at the top, which must face diagonally outward.

This will set up an even circulation of water around the aquarium. The intake port of the filter (drawing in dirty water) is right on the bottom of the unit, so take care not to bury it in the substrate, as this will drastically reduce the filter's performance.

Regular maintenance is vital to ensure that the solid waste trapped in the filter foam does not build up to a level that impedes the growth of filtration bacteria. (see page 152 for filter maintenance). A lack of oxygenated water will cause the bacteria to die off and the water quality will deteriorate, potentially causing lethal conditions for the fish. If these filter units are well maintained, however, they should give many years of reliable service.

### External power filters

An external filter is located outside the aquarium, with minimal pipework visible inside the tank. Being generally larger than their internal counterparts, they have a greater turnover, so can filter water in more "demanding" tanks. They have the capacity to house different media for mechanical, biological and chemical filtration. These are often housed in separate compartments inside the filter body. The incoming dirty water passes through the mechanical filter medium first — usually open cell foam — to remove solid waste. The water then passes through the biological medium, often

## An external power filter

Dirty water enters the filter by gravity, is cleaned and then pumped back to the aquarium.

Internal canister houses the different filter media arranged in layers.

Biological medium (ceramic cylinders) provides a surface on which beneficial bacteria can multiply.

Filter foam traps large pieces of debris and also acts as a biological medium .

Activated carbon removes toxic substances.

Filter floss prevents any fine particles becoming trapped in the impeller.

*Above:* Arrange the filter media in the canister, with the coarse filter foam at the bottom, followed by a layer of biological medium, then the carbon and finally a wad of filter wool.

21

ceramic hollow cylinders or a "high-tech" sintered glass medium that has been baked to a high temperature to create millions of microscopic cracks that are the ideal home for colonies of "cleansing" bacteria. The final stage is usually shared between a specific chemical medium and/or a wad of fine filter wool to trap any tiny particles of solid debris remaining in the water before it is pumped back to the aquarium.

The flow rate from an external filter is governed by how far it is below the water surface and the length of its hose. For the best flow, place the filter as close to the water level as possible — typically in the cabinet underneath the aquarium — and minimize the hose length. When selecting a unit, ensure that it has good-quality isolation taps, as these will be the only thing preventing a flooded room when you disconnect the filter for maintenance. Also check that the seal between the motor head and the body — usually a rubber "O" ring — is easy to locate and stays in place when you re-assemble the unit. If this seal is not located properly, the filter will leak.

## Air-powered filters

These compact internal units draw water through a small container of filter medium or a block of foam and are powered by an upward stream of bubbles supplied from an air pump. They are ideal for a quarantine or hospital tank (see page 118), where their action provides

aeration as well as filtration for new or convalescing fish. They are not suitable for a main aquarium and certainly not where carbon dioxide dosing is running to boost plant growth. The extra aeration will "gas off" the carbon dioxide before the plants have the chance to use it. (See page 25 for more details of carbon dioxide fertilization systems.)

## Hang-on power filters

A hang-on power filter works in the same way as an external power filter, except that it hangs on the edge of the aquarium glass. Water is drawn up into the unit by an impeller, passes through various types

*Above: Air-powered sponge filters are safe to use in fry-rearing tanks. Not only do they trap dirt particles, they are also colonized by micro-organisms that provide live food for young fish. They are also ideal filters for use in quarantine or treatment tanks, as shown on page 118.*

*Above: A hang-on power filter on the side of an aquarium, shown with the cover removed and the carbon-filled floss bag pulled up into view.*

of filter medium and then cascades back into the aquarium.

## Types of filter media

Mechanical filter media range from various grades of foam to very fine filter floss. Biological filtration media include sintered glass and ceramic cylinders. Chemical media are used as short-term solutions to water quality problems.

**Open cell foam** is used in both internal and external power filters. It provides a huge internal surface area on which beneficial bacteria can grow. It also functions as an excellent mechanical filter medium but needs regular cleaning to ensure that the core does not become clogged with debris. With time, foam will shrink and lose its shape and will need replacing. It is a good idea to replace only half the foam at a time to ensure that you do not lose all your filtration bacteria at once. Test the water for a few days after each change of filter foam, as the initial reduction in bacterial population may allow the water quality to deteriorate.

*Above: Maintenance on an internal cartridge filter is a simple process of replacing the pads.*

*Above: This model has two cartridges, one to purify the water and another to strain algae.*

**Ceramic cylinders** form a good biological filter medium in an external power filter, having a large surface area for bacteria and an open structure allowing plenty of water flow. Unlike foam, ceramic cylinders are relatively easy to clean by gently agitating in old aquarium water and only need replacing every few years.

**Sintered glass** is a high-capacity biological filter medium manufactured at extremely high temperatures to create microscopic cracks in the surface of the fragments. This massive surface area not only supports aerobic nitrifying bacteria (that break down ammonia and nitrites into much less toxic nitrates), but also anaerobic reduction bacteria that break down nitrates into completely harmless nitrogen gas. Use sintered glass exclusively as a biological medium, and provide excellent mechanical filtration for the water reaching it. Any prolonged buildup of solid debris will render the microscopic cracks useless as sites for efficient biological filtration.

**Plastic media** is specifically designed to have a lot of surface area. In some media the structures are quite coarse so they act as mechanical filtration and capture large particles of waste. Other types of plastic media, often called "bio-balls," are designed more for biological filtration. Both types are very durable and, with regular maintenance, will provide long-term filtration.

**Activated carbon** has been used as a filter medium for many years but only recently have we understood how it works. Activated carbons from different sources, such as bone, coconut or coal, have different characteristics and perform certain aquarium roles better than others. The most efficient option, therefore, is a blend of carbons from various sources. The active sites on the carbon absorb (take up on the surface) impurities from the water and so carbon is useful

***Activated carbon** blended from a variety of sources is the most effective for aquarium use.*

***Filter wool** removes fine particles and "polishes" the water before it is finally returned to the tank.*

***Sintered glass cylinders** provide a huge surface area for beneficial bacteria to colonize.*

***Plastic media** such as these sturdy "bio-balls" are ideal for mechanical and biological filtration.*

***Gravel** plays a part in mechanical and biological filtration but is not as efficient as other media.*

***Chemical filter media** have specific purposes, such as removing nitrates or phosphates.*

for removing substances such as dyes, leftover medications and organic wastes. Change your carbon every month to six weeks, and always rinse it under the tap before use to remove any fine dust.

**Chemical filter media** are usually specific ion-exchange resins that pick up a particular chemical in the water and swap it for a harmless salt. These media are very fast acting and are mostly used to remove nitrates or phosphates. Always use them along with a test kit to monitor the levels of the chemical you are trying to eliminate. Remove chemical media before treating the tank with medications.

**Filter wool** is ideal as the last stage of filtration to remove fine particles and add a final "polish" to the water before it returns to the aquarium. Use it either loose or in pad form and check it regularly, as once it becomes clogged it will let very little water through. It is difficult to clean without destroying the structure of the material. The best option is simply to use a new batch of this inexpensive filter medium each time.

## Fitting a heater-thermostat

Once the filter is in place, the heater is the next bit of equipment to install. Heater-thermostats, or "heaterstats," are needed in the aquarium to maintain a constant, stable temperature; for most tropical aquarium fish the ideal range is between 24°C and 26°C (75°F–78°F) All heaterstats have a dial that allows you to set the desired temperature and should, under normal conditions, maintain the aquarium at the set temperature.

## Traditional heaterstats

Most heaterstats are made of two halves contained within a single glass tube, the heating element and the thermostat. The thermostat measures the water temperature and if it drops below the desired setting, power is supplied to the heating element. Heating elements are usually made from metal, with ceramic parts to distribute heat evenly, and vary in length depending on the power of the heater and the volume of water that needs heating. Standard sizes range from 25 watts for very small aquariums, usually no more than 50 liters (13 gallons), up to 300 watts for aquariums up to 300–400 liters (79–105 gallons). For larger tanks, it is a good idea to use two heaters so that neither is working to full capacity and one will heat the water if the other should fail for any reason.

The heaterstat should be positioned at a 45-degree angle, with the heating end pointing downward. This allows the best dissipation of heat without newly heated water affecting the thermostat end of the heater. Ideally, the heaterstat should be placed in an area of good water flow, such as near the filter, and several centimeters below the surface so that it is not exposed during routine water changes. If the heaterstat is switched on while out of water, it can overheat and crack, so it is vital that it is only switched on once in position and fully submerged.

Some traditional heaterstats have electronic thermostats that will keep the temperature stable within one degree, safety shut-off switches and toughened glass to resist cracking.

## Modern heaterstats

Technological advancements through the use of microchip control and modern materials have resulted in a number of new heaterstat designs on the market, which offer many improvements over the traditional heaterstat. New electronics have given better accuracies over temperature control, better displays to show how hard the heater is working, and better safety, with immediate shut-offs if the heater is exposed to air. The new models of heaterstats cost more than the traditional designs, but offer better temperature control and are much safer to use.

**Left:** A reliable heaterstat is an essential piece of kit. Choose a sturdy model with an easy-to-read temperature scale and precise adjustment control.

**Left:** Most heater thermostats can be set to maintain a temperature between 18°C and 32°C (64°F–90°F). They are generally preset to 27°C (80°F), but are easy to adjust by turning a knob.

**Below:** Although it is more expensive, a modern heaterstat, such as this solid ceramic heater, is virtually unbreakable, offers better temperature control, and has many extra features.

## Carbon dioxide fertilization

For plants to flourish in the aquarium they require three things: nutrients, light and carbon dioxide ($CO_2$). Nutrients will be added with the substrate and lighting will be discussed later. For now, we will focus on adding $CO_2$.

Plants use $CO_2$ (a gas) and light to make sugars for energy and growth through the process of photosynthesis. $CO_2$ and light must be in balance: if there is excess $CO_2$ and not enough light to "use it up" through photosynthesis, it could encourage algae, affect the water quality, and potentially harm fish and other livestock in the aquarium. On the other hand, if there is insufficient $CO_2$ then even the brightest lighting will not result in abundant plant growth.

It is not essential to add $CO_2$: all living things in the aquarium (such as fish, filter bacteria, even plants) release $CO_2$ through the process of respiration. However, there will not be a great deal of $CO_2$ and so these aquariums will only support a few plants, or very slow-growing plants. Also, the lighting should be of lower intensity since the plants will not be photosynthesising very rapidly, which precludes the use of many plant species that require higher light levels.

The aquarium featured here already has a layer of nutritious plant substrate. By adding good lighting and $CO_2$ we can create an aquarium packed with plants that will grow rapidly, thrive, and look fantastic. Planted aquariums are very popular and there has been a surge in products for generating $CO_2$ that differ in their sophistication, ease of use or automation, how they generate $CO_2$, and, of course, cost.

Plants only use carbon dioxide when there is light to convert it into sugars; if $CO_2$ is added constantly even when there is no light, then levels of the gas can build up in the water, leading to water quality issues and severe damage to aquarium livestock. So $CO_2$ must only be added when the aquarium lights are on. There are different ways to achieve

## Introducing $CO_2$ gas

*The unit will start to produce $CO_2$ gas in about 24 hours and last for up to six weeks before a refill kit of sugar and blended yeasts is needed. The 24-hour break required to restart $CO_2$ generation will not cause the aquarium plants any harm.*

*Plug the pump into the same timer as the aquarium lights to ensure dosing only occurs when the lights are on and the plants are actively photosynthesising.*

*Yeast and sugar solution produce $CO_2$ gas.*

*Silicone tube carries $CO_2$ gas into the tank.*

*Small electric water pump creates water flow to distribute $CO_2$ gas.*

*Gentle streams of gas bubbles flow into the water.*

*IMPORTANT:
To prevent back siphoning in the event of a power outage, either place the unit above the aquarium water level or fit a check valve in the silicone tubing carrying the gas to the tank.*

this: either by manually dosing carbon dioxide (when the lights come on) or investing in an automatic system that keeps $CO_2$ concentration at a specific level and will only release it as it is used up. Alternatively, if an air pump is used at night to circulate the water, then any $CO_2$ in the water will harmlessly escape into the air. Whichever method of $CO_2$ is used, to maintain a successful aquarium it is important that the levels of dissolved carbon dioxide and pH (with which it shares an inextricable relationship) are closely monitored.

There are a few ways that $CO_2$ can be generated, but it is important that it is released into the aquarium in a very slow and steady way to allow it to dissolve into the water entirely rather than bubble up to the surface and be lost to the air. Ceramic diffusers have minute pores that release a mist of tiny bubbles into the

water, which dissolve before they reach the surface. The pores may become blocked in time and require clearing. Alternatively, there are $CO_2$ reactors that force the $CO_2$ bubbles along a maze, and while navigating through it, the gas dissolves into the water. It is also possible to connect the $CO_2$ supply to the outlet of an internal pump or filter. Carbon dioxide is drawn into the water as it is jetted out from the pump. Finally, the $CO_2$ can be released into a vessel that looks like an upturned cup; the carbon dioxide slowly dissolves where the gas meets the water. The best way for delivering the $CO_2$ will depend on what you want to see in the aquarium and how the $CO_2$ is generated in the first place.

## Carbon dioxide generator

For small aquariums up to 100 liters (26 gallons), a biological $CO_2$ generator

**Right:** *Place the pump at the opposite end of the tank from the filter to boost the circulation of water around the aquarium. Because this $CO_2$ system is pressurized, the pump can be placed at any depth without a reduction of carbon dioxide output.*

**Above:** *$CO_2$ bubbles are released from the tube. This picture shows the principle, although in reality the stream should be much gentler.*

is a low-cost solution to the problem of adding $CO_2$. In this system, yeast is mixed with sugar and water in a sealed container and a fermentation process begins when the yeast starts to convert the sugar to alcohol, giving off $CO_2$ in the process. The $CO_2$ gas is forced out of the container and along a tube into the aquarium, where it can be dissolved into the water through the use of a water pump or a diffuser. This method is very low cost; the yeast/sugar mix can be purchased as a ready-made mix or mixed manually using baking yeast and sugar. On the other hand, because it generates $CO_2$ continually, care must be taken to prevent the gas accumulating during darkness. Nevertheless, it is simple and effective and is the type of system we will be using in our example aquarium.

### Other low-tech $CO_2$ solutions

For small aquariums, there are a number of other options to introduce $CO_2$, including liquid, tablet and manual injection. Both tablet and manual injection systems work on the principle of a chamber inside the aquarium, which holds $CO_2$ gas (produced either from the tablets or by injecting from a canister) where it naturally diffuses into the water. To increase the effectiveness of this system the chamber should be positioned in an area of water flow, such as near the filter outlet, so that the gas is in contact with moving water and will dissolve more quickly. The benefit of this system is that the gas can be

controlled so that it is only present during daylight hours. Liquid carbon fertilization is a relatively new option, but there are a number of products on the market that simply require a daily dose of liquid to the aquarium. Although this is the simplest form of providing carbon for plants, it is also far less effective than using gas, but may provide a good starting point from which the fishkeeper can progress on to better alternatives.

### $CO_2$ injection systems

There are kits available that include a pressurized gas cylinder, a regulator to control the gas output, a very sensitive solenoid valve, and a delivery system. The cylinder lasts for many months before needing to be replaced or refilled. The most sophisticated sets include a microprocessor that measures the dissolved carbon dioxide in the water and regulates the gas dosing accordingly. With more simple sets, you must manually adjust the dose rate by regulating the number of $CO_2$ bubbles released per minute. The desired number of bubbles will depend on the size, planting and water chemistry of the aquarium. It is a good idea to start by following the manufacturer's recommendations and then adjust the level up or down based on the readings

**Right:** *Measuring the correct amount of $CO_2$ can be difficult, but a permanent indicator will help to prevent severe under- or overdosing.*

provided by the $CO_2$ level indicator included. Injection systems offer a very neat and efficient design and, though these systems are the most expensive, they offer a complete "plug-and-play" alternative.

**Above:** *Providing good illumination, plenty of nutrients and $CO_2$ fertilization will encourage strong plant growth.*

**Above:** *Using a bubble counter like this one attached to the outside of the aquarium allows you to hide internal equipment and still see how much $CO_2$ is entering the aquarium.*

**Right:** *Cylinders containing compressed $CO_2$ are ideal for larger aquariums and long-term $CO_2$ fertilization. The gas produced is sent to a bubble counter, where it is kept in contact with the water for an extended time.*

## CO₂ cylinder fertilization

*Cylinder systems can be connected to a light timer so that gas is only released when the lights are switched on. Plants have no use for $CO_2$ at night and an excess at night can harm the aquarium.*

*This valve closes when the lights are off, preventing the release of $CO_2$ gas.*

*The aquarium lights provide an energy source for photosynthesis.*

*The cylinder contains compressed $CO_2$ gas, which is released at a controlled rate via a regulator. The two dials indicate the release rate and the pressure of the gas in the cylinder, which reflects the amount of gas remaining.*

*The bubble counter allows tiny $CO_2$ bubbles to travel slowly upward, allowing maximum time for the gas to diffuse into the water.*

*Connectors and valves are standard fit and suitable for all systems.*

**Right:** *Carbon dioxide gas enters at the bottom of this diffuser. After a running-in period of about 48 hours, the bubbles stabilize and become smaller as they rise and release $CO_2$ gas into the aquarium water.*

# PREPARING AND ADDING WOOD

Wood and bamboo are popular items of aquarium decor that simulate natural features from various different habitats around the world. Wood should be purchased from an aquarium shop, where you can be sure that it will be suitable for underwater use. Wood from any other source is best avoided, as it will quickly rot and may release chemicals that could be detrimental to the health of your fish and plants. If you have any doubts about the source of any wood, you should seal it with clear plastic paint normally used for sealing concrete ponds. This product is safe to use with fish and plants. It not only prevents any harmful substances leaching into the aquarium, but it also stops the wood from rotting. Several coats may be required to achieve a good seal. Make sure the wood is completely dry before you paint it. The sealing process may give it a slightly shiny appearance, but this will soften over time as the bogwood takes on a natural look.

Aquarium wood is available in many sizes, shapes and colors, and a good aquarium store will offer a wide selection of pieces. A popular type is from the Manzanita tree, which has interesting, delicate branches and will not degrade underwater. Alternatively, there is Mopani wood or bogwood, which tends to be in more solid shapes than Manzanita. Sometimes, wood might have to be prepared for up to a couple of weeks before using it in an aquarium (see below). This helps to leach out any tannins in the water and saturates the wood so it sinks. If you find that after preparation the wood still floats, there are a couple of steps you can take to anchor it securely.

One method is to tie the wood with thin nylon fishing line to a stone that will

**Above:** *Brush the wood to remove dirt and debris. Wet it to remove stubborn marks and use a smaller brush to get into the narrow crevices.*

be hidden from view. Alternatively, use silicone to adhere the wood to a piece of glass and then bury the glass in the aquarium gravel. Any obvious connections can be easily disguised with planting.

With the wood in place, stand back

**Below:** *Place the bogwood into clean water in a bucket deep enough for the wood to remain submerged. Weight it down if it floats.*

*After several days you will notice that the water has started to discolor. Leave the bogwood submerged in the bucket.*

*When the water looks like strong tea, replace it with fresh tap water. Repeat the process as often as necessary to remove most of the tannins.*

*It may take up to two weeks and several changes of water before the water remains clear. At this point, you can place the clean, waterlogged bogwood into the aquarium.*

*Some woods will continually produce tannins for many months even after soaking, but the discoloration is not harmful and can be removed by using carbon in the filter.*

and take a look at it, ideally from the angle at which you will normally view the aquarium. This will enable you to see if it looks natural and whether you are happy with its position in the overall display.

## Preparing wood

There are many types of wood available, which differ in the amount of preparation they require. Always ask your local aquatics supplier if the wood you are buying needs pre-treating, particularly soaking. The reason for soaking the wood is that it contains large quantities of natural humic acids and tannins. If you simply place the wood into the aquarium, these naturally occurring chemicals will leach out into the water and stain it a tea-brown color. The chemicals are not harmful, but most fishkeepers prefer to keep the water as clear as possible.

To prepare bogwood, first brush it thoroughly to remove any dust and dirt. Then place it in a bucket of water,

*Right: Bed the wood into the substrate. In this setup, there is a piece on each side. Use them to hide aquarium equipment, allowing access to heaters and filters. According to their shape, arrange the pieces so that they resemble tree roots and stumps or fallen branches.*

*Below: Manzanita wood is increasing in popularity for aquarium decoration because it will not leach tannins into the water. It does float, however, and so needs soaking first.*

## Types of wood

*Bogwood is available in many shapes and sizes. If a piece is too large for your tank or has a sharp corner, break it with your hands for a natural finish.*

*Twisted roots are thinner pieces of wood that can represent overhanging branches or roots growing in a riverbank.*

*Mopani wood is pre-cleaned and has a different texture on each side.*

*Cork bark is occasionally available, but will need anchoring to keep it from floating.*

making sure it is totally submerged. Leave it for several days so that the tannins are released. If the wood floats, simply place a heavy object on top to keep it submerged. Once waterlogged, it will not float when you put it in the aquarium. The water in the bucket will gradually discolor until it resembles strong, dark tea. At this point, discard it and replace it with a fresh supply. Repeat the process until the water remains clear for several days. The wood is now ready to use.

Even though you have presoaked the bogwood, tannins will slowly continue to leach into the aquarium and these will gradually cause the pH level of the water to drop. This is something you can monitor with the help of a pH test kit (see page 94), but a maintenance routine that includes regular water changes should prevent any problems.

## Bamboo

The sealing process described for wood on page 28 is also suitable for two other types of wood that you can use in the aquarium, namely bamboo and cork bark. With its unique shape and texture, bamboo is a striking decor material and can provide excellent cover for many aquarium fish. It is available from aquatic and garden centers in various diameters. To anchor the bamboo, you may need to attach it to a piece of glass. Use aquarium silicone sealant for this job as it is strong, chemically inert when dry and therefore harmless to fish and plants.

## Resin casts

There are many replicas of wood made from resin. These have the advantage of not needing any preparation, being guaranteed to sink and not changing the water chemistry at all. On the other hand, they are not available in the infinite

*Right: The shape and rough texture of this "Jati" wood, a type of bogwood, are reminiscent of fallen branches. The natural "cave" formed by the wood will be a welcome retreat for the fish. Bed down all decor securely to avoid the risk of collapse and resulting damage to the tank and its inhabitants.*

variety of shapes found in the natural product and are a little more expensive to purchase.

## Aquascaping

Developing the underwater landscape, or "aquascape," is a fun and inspiring

*Above: Left untreated, bamboo will rot in the aquarium, releasing organic elements that may cause algal or fungal blooms. Allow it to dry out completely before painting it with a sealant suitable for aquarium use.*

opportunity to build your own underwater world: the possibilities are endless, and you can create whatever effect you please. However, if you need some inspiration start by looking at aquarium displays in shops, through fishkeeping magazines, or online. If you

*Below: Thick bamboo canes, cut to different lengths, weighted down with a pebble inside, and positioned amid dense planting become distinctive items of decor in this display.*

want to create a themed aquarium, such as a shady Amazonian stream, books and magazines feature plenty of location photography of the natural habitats in which aquarium plants and fish live. They also give an indication of other appropriate decor such as wood, rocks and substrate. Often, the most successful displays are made up of a restricted palate of decor: one type of wood or stone with just a couple of bold pieces to complement the planting, rather than a lot of different pieces. In the end, of course, it is up to personal taste.

Before placing any decor in the aquarium it is a good idea to sketch out an overhead plan showing where all the elements are to go. First, incorporate all the essentials in your plan: the heaters, pipework and filters/pumps. These will ideally be hidden when looking from the front so you will want to position decor and plants accordingly. An established technique when considering the position of decor is the rule of thirds.

## The rule of thirds

For hundreds of years, artists and photographers have known that placing the focal point dead center in the frame makes for an uninteresting result. Setting it to one side breathes life and dynamism into the composition. The same rules apply when aquascaping, but where should the focal point be? Imagine dividing the aquarium roughly into thirds vertically and horizontally. The best place for a focal point is at the intersection of one of these thirds. The focal point might be represented by an interesting piece of wood or a craggy rock. In all but the largest of aquariums, it is best to have just one focal point and a secondary complementary feature, such as a smaller rock. You may wish to set up the hard decor outside the aquarium first to see how the pieces work together, or you may wish to do this directly within the aquarium. Always start with the largest piece of decor as your main focal point.

## Dutch and Japanese style

There are two basic "schools" in planted aquariums. The Dutch style (named after its origins) is the oldest and excludes all decor in order to cram in more plants. The planting is done in blocks, much like a flower border in the garden and, like a border, features a wide variety of plants. The Japanese style is much more restricted; it features a couple of very carefully considered rocks, artfully arranged, and a narrow range of plants. Often the effect can resemble a tiny world, with fish appearing to fly through the canopy of plants. Both of these styles are very specific in what they will allow, so most people take a bit of what they like from each.

Whatever style you choose, make sure the gravel slopes from deep at the back to shallower at the front. This ensures that waste will gradually roll down the slope to the front of the aquarium, where you can see and remove it.

### Creating a realistic display

- Rock strata should run in the same direction. Vertical strata can look unnatural, horizontal might "flatten" the look, but diagonal can work well.
- All decor must be very secure, with no risk of it floating. Avoid creating unbalanced structures and do not lean heavy rocks against the aquarium glass.
- Use the full height of the aquarium. Ideally, the decor should fill the height of the tank to create all-round interest and make full use of the space available.
- Low-lying wood and rocks can be used to create banks of substrate or to define plant-growing areas.
- Use decor to hide aquarium equipment.
- Avoid a central "pyramid" layout. It often ends up looking like just a pile of rocks!
- Consider whether your layout creates "dead-zones" where you cannot see food and waste accumulating. For example, the intersection between three stones is impossible to clean or check for gathering waste.
- Empty space is a good thing! It represents growing room for the plants, swimming area for fish, and somewhere to rest the eyes before appreciating all the other details.

## A basic plan

*Mark in where all the equipment is to go. This is the water pump connected to the CO$_2$ fertilizer unit.*

*Sketch in the intended location of the rocks you propose to use.*

*Include the filter and heaterstat in a position where they can be easily accessed for routine maintenance.*

*Mark in the location of the wood pieces. Leave an open swimming space for the fish.*

# CHOOSING ROCKS

Aquarium shops carry a selection of rocks, but not all of them are suitable for the freshwater tropical community display we are creating here. As with the substrate, the requirement is for inert materials that will not affect the water chemistry. Ideal rocks include basalt, flint, slate, sandstone, quartz and lava rock. Unsuitable materials include limestone, marble and chalk. Avoid these calcareous rocks, as they will continually raise the pH of the water in the aquarium by releasing calcium salts.

Do not collect rocks from the wild, as you may not be able to identify them and, again, they could alter the water chemistry in the aquarium (see page 34). Here we look at a range of rocks that are suitable.

**Pebbles** are an excellent addition to the display. They have a natural riverbed appearance and are ideal for creating a textural difference in the foreground. They can also be used as a dividing line between two vigorous foreground plants, such as *Glossostigma elatinoides* and *Echinodorus tenellus*.

**Lava rock** can be used in large pieces to create a completely different look. With this material you can create a backdrop that is ideal for growing plants such as Java Fern (*Microsorium pteropus*), *Anubias barteri* var. *nana* and liverwort (*Monosolenium tenerum*). The roots of these plants have no problem anchoring themselves securely onto the open, porous structure of the lava rock. It is always worth running your hand carefully over the lava rock surface before placing it in the aquarium to check for very sharp edges that could injure the fish. They will be difficult to remove later on, so knock them off now with a hammer.

**Coal** is an unusual addition choice of decor, but can look very effective. Wash it thoroughly before use — a messy business that may persuade you to use another material.

**Westmorland rock** is an attractive addition to the aquascaping armory, although not the cheapest rock to buy. The red-brown color and striated markings make it a distinctive alternative for use in, for example, a brackish aquarium display.

**Slate** is commonly available and can look stunning. Use the flat, purple-gray pieces to create some interesting aquarium features, such as a natural cave. Place a piece of slate onto the substrate, leaving just a small gap underneath and any fish with a slight burrowing instinct will shape the substrate to their own requirements.

## Types of rock

Granite has an unusual sparkling texture and will appear more natural with time.

Slate is available in a range of shapes and sizes. Position this heavy rock with care.

Rounded boulders have a great impact in aquarium displays and make good grazing spots for algae-eaters.

Westmorland rock has an attractive reddish color and striking markings.

Chippings are available for many rock types. These are slate pieces.

Broken pieces of lava rock create an unusual substrate.

Washed coal is a good choice for creating a darker display.

Small rounded pebbles are ideal for creating a riverbed.

**Granite, flint and sandstone** are all inert rocks for use in the aquarium. You can combine smaller chippings with large pieces for extra effect. If your aquarium shop only has a limited selection of pieces, consider a visit to a local gardening center for more choice. Apart from an aquarium shop, this will be the only place where you can be sure of what you are buying.

## Artificial decor

Finally, do not overlook the range of artificial decor available. Modern products look very realistic, as the molds used are often taken from real pieces of wood or rock. The paint finishes are excellent and you can build up a very realistic backdrop using these pieces. Many have also been developed to hide specific items of equipment inside the aquarium.

*Artificial wood looks natural and does not alter the color of the water.*

*This fake bark is a good shape for hiding internal filters.*

**Above:** *Individually, these pebbles and stones make good aquarium decor, but used together, they have greater impact.*

**Below:** *Combining artificial pieces of decor with genuine rocks and plants help them to appear more authentic. Here the large and small rocks and pebbles are real, but the "wood" is synthetic.*

*Synthetic rock is inert and safe for any aquarium.*

*Fake wood is available in manageable sizes.*

## Choosing and using rocks

When selecting rock, take time to examine several pieces and arrange them to see how they look together. If the rock has visible strata, the golden rule is that all the lines should run in the same direction. Arranged properly in the aquarium, they will have the appearance of a natural river- or lake-bed. As with bogwood, rocks can be positioned to define different areas of the aquarium and to form a natural divide between plants.

If you are unsure about the suitability of a rock, then a simple vinegar test will put your mind at ease. Simply place a few drops of malt vinegar onto a clean area of the rock surface. If the vinegar begins to fizz, it is the result of a chemical reaction between the acidic vinegar and the calcareous material of the rock.

## Preparing rocks

Before using any rocks in the aquarium, scrub them to remove dust and debris. Clean, wet rock shows its true colors under aquarium lighting. Dirty rock looks out of place underwater; in the natural world, it would have had many years of washing. Dust from rocks will also cloud the water, which spoils the overall effect.

## Testing rocks for suitability

To test if a rock is likely to alter the water chemistry, pour on an acidic substance such as vinegar. If the rock contains any calcareous substances, it will begin to fizz gently. If there is no fizzing it should be safe to use in the aquarium. You may need to examine the rock carefully for the bubbles that appear when an acid is added to an alkaline rock.

*Below:* Rocks are not only dirty and dusty, they may also harbour mosses and lichens that could foul the water. Scrub them thoroughly before adding them to the tank.

You may prefer to wear rubber gloves while you scrub the rocks.

Low-pressure $CO_2$ fertilization system

A small brush with stiff bristles will penetrate all the crevices.

Wash the rocks in clean water. Working over a bucket minimizes the risk of splashing water on the floor if you are working indoors.

Pre-washed rock

Heaterstat

Internal power filter

**Above:** *Decide where the rocks are going. If you are following a plan on paper, refer to it as you work. When you are satisfied, seat the rock into place. Never lean rocks against the glass or place them onto the glass base. Small pieces of gravel will be pressed into the glass and smash it. Do not create a pile of rocks, as gaps in it will harbor waste that will be difficult to remove.*

**Left:** *Tall rocks are useful for hiding unsightly equipment. Lower heavy pieces carefully into the tank to avoid damaging the glass. Make sure they are stable and secure.*

# TREATING AND ADDING WATER

Only when you have installed all the aquarium equipment and are completely happy with the layout of the rocks, bogwood and other decor, is it time to fill the tank with water. Do not add plants at this point, as most require the support of the water to stay upright and in any case, the filling process would dislodge them.

## Conditioning the water

As we discuss on page 90, tap water is ideal for the aquarium, providing it is first treated with a proprietary water conditioner to remove chemicals that would otherwise harm the plants and fish. A product that also contains beneficial bacteria will help to trigger biological cycles in the aquarium. Following the manufacturer's instructions, simply add the whole of the required amount of liquid water conditioner to the first bucketful of tap water before filling the aquarium.

## Final checks

Before you start to fill the aquarium, make sure that it has not been knocked slightly out of place during the first phase of setting up. A tank that overhangs the base, even by a small amount, is both unsightly and dangerous, and the situation will be impossible to rectify when the tank is full of water. Double check that the tank is level and that you are happy with the equipment installed so far. Once you start filling it, the aquarium will become impossible to move. Filling can be a messy business, so make sure you have a towel on hand ready to mop up any spills.

*Below: Pour the conditioned water carefully from the bucket onto a saucer, flat stone or even a plastic bag to prevent the water splashing. If you prefer, start filling the tank with a plastic jug and progress to a bucket when the water level has started to rise.*

## Measuring the tank volume

Filling the aquarium with a bucket of a known capacity enables you to measure the volume of water in the aquarium accurately. Although it is easy to calculate the volume of a rectangular aquarium, this does not take into account the displacement of the gravel, decor and equipment. Using a bucket, you can measure the volume of water precisely. When the aquarium is roughly two-thirds full, record the water volume so far. It is important to know exactly how much water the aquarium holds, because at some future date you may have to treat sick fish with medication diluted according to the volume of the aquarium. Accurate dosage is vital; underdosing may not kill the disease organism you are treating and overdosing can quite easily kill your fish.

*Above: Using a tap water conditioner is a quick and reliable method of neutralizing the chemicals added to make the water suitable for human consumption. It is then safe to use in the aquarium.*

**Above:** *Depending on how much access the hood gives you, it may be easier to remove it while you are filling the tank. Make a note of how much water is going in the tank for future reference.*

*Filling the tank to this level minimizes the risk of water overflowing when you introduce the plants.*

**Below:** *Continue filling the tank until it is half to three-quarters full. Make sure the heater and filter intake are fully submerged. Switch on the filter overnight to heat and clear the water. The water is bound to look cloudy at first.*

## Filling the aquarium

As you fill the tank, it is important not to disturb the carefully washed gravel and layer of planting substrate. To avoid too much splashing caused by a strong flow of water from a bucket, place a plate or a thick plastic bag onto the gravel and slowly pour the water onto the plate or bag. This will help to spread out the water and minimize any disturbance.

Initially, you should only fill the aquarium to half of its full capacity. This will leave plenty of room for water movement and displacement when you put your arms in the tank to plant it up. The water you have put in will be sufficient to support the plants once they are in position.

# PREPARING TO PLANT THE AQUARIUM

Now that the bare bones of the aquarium are in place, the enjoyable task of completing the aquascaping can continue. Overnight, the filter will have cleared any haziness from the water and the heater will have warmed the water to its preset temperature. The result is a clean and comfortable environment in which to build up the display.

Before proceeding with any planting, it is worth returning to your basic plan of the aquarium and sketching in where the plants are to go (see page 40). Keep the plants in their transportation bags until you are ready to use them. In this way, they will remain in a moist environment and will not suffer too much from drying out, which can quickly happen in a warm house. Each plant can then be dealt with in turn, without being exposed to the drying air for too long. Start by adding the background plants and working forward to complete the display.

Here are a few final tips before you begin planting. Wear short sleeves when undertaking any tasks that involve putting your hands in the tank. Keep a towel within easy reach, as your arms will be constantly in and out of the aquarium, which can lead to plenty of drips and a soggy carpet. If you have sensitive skin, consider wearing rubber gloves to prevent any problems arising from prolonged contact with the water. Finally, keep a waste bucket close by so that you can easily dispose of packaging materials, plant baskets and unwanted leaves.

By the end of the day you should have an immature but complete planting display that is ready to flourish under your guidance.

*After 24 hours, the water will have settled and cleared and the aquarium is ready for plants. Later in this section you will find a selection of plants for all areas of the display.*

# Choosing plants

Faced with an extensive choice of plants, your first consideration must be the size of your aquarium and the type of display you want to create. Although you may love a particular plant, there is no point in including it if it will outgrow your aquarium in six months time. Some aquariums look stunning with minimal planting in a "geological display" dominated by rocks and bogwood, while others are totally plant filled, with no other decor visible among the foliage. Both displays can be equally effective, even though they are completely different. Or you may want to recreate a natural habitat, such as an Asian stream, using only the plants and fish that are found together in the wild.

Often, plants look more dramatic when planted in groups, so buy several of a few varieties rather than many species.

Also, consider your system: will it have carbon dioxide added? How bright is the lighting? Some plants need both these things to grow. Your retailer will advise you on the range of plants that will thrive in your aquarium conditions.

## Making a plan

On page 31 we discussed sketching out an overhead plan of the aquarium showing where all the major items of equipment and hard decor should go. You can take this idea a step further by also making a planting plan in the same way that you would design garden beds. With the fixed "hard landscaping" in place, you can see how much room is left for plants and where the planting areas occur.

You can divide the plan to create background, midground and foreground areas. These are not intended to be strict lines within which to plant, but they will be useful as a guide to help you design the display. To achieve a natural tiered effect, envision your plan from the front to the back, with the shortest plants in the center foreground and the tallest ones at the back. You don't need to stick to this rule too rigidly; nature doesn't. A tall plant or two in the midground makes you wonder what might be behind, and you can enjoy seeing fish swim around the plants as they navigate their way through the display. The finished effect should look natural, with plants overlapping and not arranged like a regimented flowerbed. Be flexible with your planting scheme and make sure you leave enough room for each plant to mature and grow. If the display is crammed full of plants from the outset, they will simply outgrow the space and the weaker ones will die. Turn to the plant section beginning on page 52 to find out how much room each plant will need. Once you have this information, you can begin to choose suitable plants for each of the three main planting areas.

## Buying plants

You do not have to buy all your plants at the same time, but the aquarium display will look more complete if you can finish the planting all at once.

Most good aquatic retailers have a wide range of tropical aquarium plants, which should be displayed in easy-to-view, clean tanks. Plants should be labelled with details of their mature height and spread, price, and ideally, a guide to the best planting position in the aquarium:

*Right: When you buy new plants, each one should be packed in a plastic bag with plenty of air inside to prevent crushing during transit. The bags need not contain water; sealing them is enough to retain moisture.*

## A planting plan for your aquarium

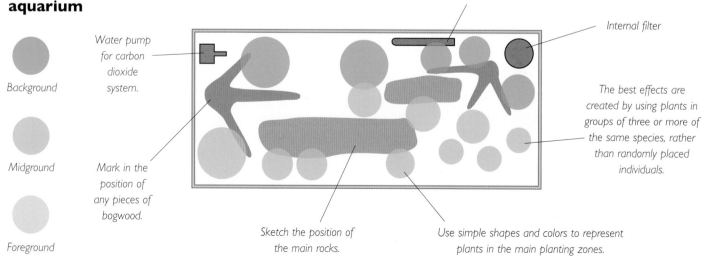

Background

Midground

Foreground

Water pump for carbon dioxide system.

Mark in the position of any pieces of bogwood.

Heaterstat

Internal filter

The best effects are created by using plants in groups of three or more of the same species, rather than randomly placed individuals.

Sketch the position of the main rocks.

Use simple shapes and colors to represent plants in the main planting zones.

## Choosing healthy plants

Good-quality plants will repay you by establishing quickly and making strong, healthy new growth. Examine plants carefully and reject poor specimens.

**Left:** *Leaves with no holes, plus roots and small plantlets growing through the base of the pot, are evidence of a healthy plant.*

**Above:** *Buying plants directly from a retailer enables you to pick out the species you need and examine individual specimens. However, the range of plants may be limited and you may have to visit several suppliers to locate all your chosen plants.*

**Right:** *Avoid plants with brown or damaged leaves. They will rot away in the aquarium. Yellow patches, particularly toward the leaf edge, indicate a lack of nutrients.*

background, midground, etc. If a certain species has any special care requirements, these should also be made clear.

It is vital to start with strong, healthy plants. Weak, sickly specimens are unlikely to recover fully, will probably die and generally look unsightly. Always choose plants with evidence of strong new growth and avoid those with many yellowing, blotched or damaged leaves.

Most plants are sold either as potted specimens or in bunches of individual stems secured in a foam-lined lead strip.

**Above:** *It is vital that mail-order plants are well protected during their journey. Here, they are packed in separate bags, placed in a polystyrene box and wrapped in several layers of bubblewrap.*

**Left:** *Unpack each plant but leave it in its bag until you are ready to use it. Check the plants against your order. It may be worth ordering more than you need in case of any losses in transit.*

41

The lead ensures that they sink and are displayed effectively in the aquarium shop. Carefully examine bunched plants and reject any that have been damaged by crushing, as they will take a long time to recover.

In potted plants, you can often see new growth appearing through the sides of the containers — a sign that the plants are in excellent condition. If the roots are visible, they should be white and healthy. Inspect the roots of any plants growing in substrate before committing to buy them.

When you have chosen your plants, the retailer should place them in plastic bags that are then filled with air, which prevents the leaves from being crushed during transit. A good retailer will package your plants with care and you should reject any that appear to have been damaged by rough handling.

Once you reach home, transfer the plants into the aquarium as soon as possible. If your tank has only recently been set up, make sure the water temperature is at least 25°C (77°F), otherwise temperature shock will damage the plants.

## Mail order plants

There is a huge range of suppliers on the internet and many advertise in aquatics magazines. If possible, ask other hobbyists for recommendations or read the reports in the magazines to check on the service of the companies and the quality of the plants on sale. The benefit of shopping online is that the best suppliers are specialists who provide a full description of each plant and its needs. Often, they will have collections for certain conditions, such as "need bright lighting," "carpet forming," or "red-leaved."

The risk is that you cannot see the specimen you are buying; less reputable suppliers will send plants that are very small or lack established root systems (though such companies are very much the exception these days). It is worth noting the company's policy if you are dissatisfied with the plants when they arrive. Before ordering, make sure you will be available to accept delivery on the day and that the tank is completely ready: plants left in the package for a day or weekend will take a long time to recover from the journey. When the plants are delivered, they should be carefully wrapped in plastic bags, surrounded with insulation material and packed in a sturdy box for protection. Leave them in the bags until you place them in the aquarium as they will quickly dry out when unwrapped.

## Preparing for planting

Good preparation before planting will ensure that plants get a good start in life and grow strongly.

## Preparing Echinodorus

*This healthy plant is* Echinodorus *"Red Special." The roots are growing strongly through the rockwool medium and out of the base of the pot — always a good sign. Keep any labels that you remove from the pots in a safe place. You may need them for future reference.*

**1** *Begin by removing the plastic container. Cut the sides of the pot, in several place if necessary, until you can remove it easily and without damaging the plant.*

**2** *Carefully peel away the pot to reveal the rockwool growing medium. Sometimes it is possible to remove the pot simply by squeezing it gently and sliding out the plant.*

**Potted plants** The first task is to remove potted plants from their plastic containers. If squeezing the container is not enough to release the plant, cut away the pot and separate it from the root structure. If necessary, cut the pot into pieces to make it easier to remove. Handle the plants with utmost care to avoid damaging delicate stems and roots.

Potted plants are much cheaper but not as well established and will take longer to create an effect.

Most potted plants are grown in a rockwool medium that supplies them with nutrients while they are in the nursery. However, once in the aquarium, they will obtain all the nutrients they require from the substrate and a regular program of fertilization. Before planting, you should remove as much rockwool from the roots as you can. Peel it away carefully. If some pieces are difficult to reach, leave them in place, as it is not worth damaging the plant just to remove a small piece of rockwool that will eventually be buried in the aquarium.

Once you have removed the pot and the rockwool, examine the plant carefully.

Healthy roots should be white and strong. Trim off any with minor damage using a sharp knife or scissors. If you leave them on they will die and decay in the substrate. Remove any leaves that are past their best or have been accidentally damaged in transit. Take off yellowing leaves or any with holes in, again using sharp scissors or a knife to ensure a clean cut.

**Bunched plants** The lead strips holding bunches of stems in place are not needed in the home aquarium, so undo them carefully and discard them. You could return the strips to the aquarium shop for reuse to avoid dumping them into the environment. Separate out large-leaved plants supplied in bunches and place them into the aquarium in a small group. Long-stemmed, small-leaved aquarium plants look much better if planted relatively close together as a bunch.

## Planting
Placing plants in the aquarium takes a bit of practice. If you are inexperienced, the easiest way is to use both hands.

## Preparing Glossostigma

*Glossostigma elatinoides is a tiny foreground plant that only grows to 2–3 cm (0.8–1.2 in) tall. It requires careful handling.*

*Remove as much rockwool as you can without causing damage. If this is too difficult, expose only the base of the roots, leaving the remaining rockwool intact.*

3 *Remove as much of the growing medium from the roots as you can, taking care not to damage the roots. This can be quite tricky, so take your time.*

4 *If the roots are too long, trim them with sharp scissors so that you can spread them out when you come to plant them. Roots planted in a bunch may rot.*

5 *Check over the plant and remove any old or damaged leaves. Make sure there are no snails or evidence of snails eggs. These appear as blobs of jelly on the leaves.*

Hold the base of the plant in one hand, carefully supporting the leaves with your fingers, scoop a hole in the gravel with the other hand and gently push the plant into the hole so that its roots are in the nutrient layer and the crown is just above the finished substrate level. Backfill the hole with the excavated substrate. Avoid disturbing the substrate too much, as you will also move the nutrient layer. Try to work fairly rapidly, as any hole made in an underwater substrate tends to fill up again quite quickly.

**Below:** *Prepare each plant as described on pages 42–43. Working across the back of the tank, begin to put in the plants. This is one of two Echinodorus cordifolius ssp. fluitans that will occupy the back lefthand corner.*

If possible, learn to work one-handed. Holding the plant as before, use one or two fingers to make the planting hole and then push in the plant immediately and backfill with gravel.

When you have decided on the position of the plant in the aquarium, make sure it looks roughly as you imagined. Several

replantings will damage the plant and extend its settling-in period. Remember that if the odd leaf looks out of place, it will change position as the plant responds to its new light source over the next few days.

**Right:** *Moving along to the center back, the next plant to go in is Echinodorus "Red Special." It will develop into a good specimen plant, is not difficult to look after and grows reasonably quickly.*

When adding plants, be careful not to dislodge items you have already positioned.

*Left:* In the right-hand corner, three Echinodorus "Red Flame" complete the background. Look at the aquarium from the front to make sure you are happy with the position of the plants.

*Below:* Make sure that each plant has its roots in the nutrient layer of the substrate so that it can obtain maximum benefit. Although you must treat the plants gently, firm them into the substrate so that they do not tilt or fall over.

## Background planting

Following the plan you have drawn up, start planting from one corner to the other across the back of the aquarium and then work forward in the same way to complete the planting.

For the background of this aquarium display, we have chosen three varieties of Amazon swordplant. The first is *Echinodorus cordifolius,* a large, bright green species that will eventually fill the rear lefthand corner and conceal the carbon dioxide pump as it grows. Two plants will begin to form the frame, softening the hard edges of the aquarium and helping the bogwood to blend into the display.

The center of the background is often a key location for a specimen plant. We are using *Echinodorus* "Red Special," which has contrasting red-and-green leaves that will create a superb backdrop.

The righthand side of this display is dominated by the upright rock, the heaterstat and the internal filter. Although it is important to retain access to the equipment, there is nothing to prevent the development of large-leaved plants that will effectively disguise the hardware when the display is viewed from the front. Three smaller specimens of the stunning Amazon swordplant *Echinodorus* "Red Flame" are planted in an L-shape around the corner of the tank so they grow up in a group.

## Midground planting

In this display, the midground will feature one species of plant, namely *Cryptocoryne wendtii* "Tropica." Its red-and-green leaves will blend with the Amazon swordplants in the background, but will be perfectly visible, as this species only grows half as tall. The cryptocorynes will form a curtain across two-thirds of the midground, leaving the fish with a swimming area toward the lefthand side near the bogwood and at the rear of the display. Remember to leave enough growing room so that the plants do not become overcrowded. Here, the three *C. w.* "Tropica" are planted about 10 cm (4 in) apart. Planting in groups of three or five looks more natural. Of course, there are many more *Cryptocoryne* species — as well as other midground plants — from which to choose (see pages 60–73).

### Preparing Cryptocoryne

*Cryptocoryne wendtii "Tropica" has attractive, dark, textured leaves. A small group planted together will develop to form a clump in the midground.*

**1** *Having removed the plant from its pot and teased away the rockwool from the roots, trim away any yellowing or damaged leaves with sharp scissors before planting.*

**2** *This cryptocoryne is ready to plant, along with two more, in the midground. Cryptocorynes are popular aquarium plants and widely available. To prevent the risk of cryptocoryne rot, avoid fluctuations in lighting and heating conditions.*

**Right**: *Supporting the cryptocoryne with three fingers, make a hole in the substrate deep enough to accept the plant roots.*

**Above:** *Gently push the plant into the substrate, making sure that the roots are in contact with the nutrient layer. Practice working with one hand; it will prove less disruptive for the existing plants.*

**Above:** *With the plant in position, draw in the substrate around the roots to anchor it, just as if you were planting into the ground. Repeat the process with the other two cryptocorynes.*

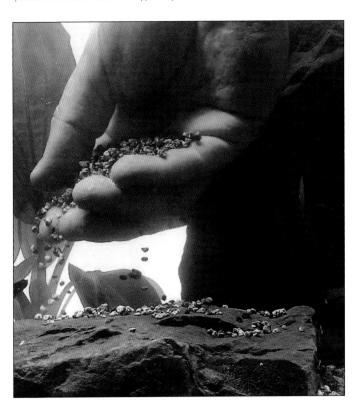

**Above:** *You may find that you need to add some additional substrate around the plants. Drop it gently into the tank. Leave enough space between the plants for them to grow and spread.*

## Foreground planting

To complete the planting of this display we need some foreground plants, and we have chosen four very different species that each make an impact in their own way. The lefthand side will feature *Hygrophila polysperma* "Rosanervig," a tall plant that reaches the water surface and needs regular clipping back to ensure that it does not overtake the display and block out light to the other foreground plants.

In the mid-foreground there will be two species: the first is *Hemianthus micranthemoides*, a bushy plant with small, fine leaves. It can grow up to 15 cm (6 in) tall, so it, too, will need clipping to ensure that it spreads along the front of the tank instead of reaching for the light. Two of them planted together will form a clump toward the front.

**Below:** Hygrophila polysperma *is the choice for the lefthand corner, in front of* Echinodorus cordifolius ssp fluitans. *This end-on view shows the* Hygrophila *being offered up into position.*

Slightly right of center is a liverwort, which adds another leaf texture at the front of the display. Like most liverworts, this one does not root into the substrate, but is supplied attached by netting to a rock or purpose-made planting stone. Simply place this on the substrate and the plant will soon cover the entire stone and the netting. The effect is of an anchored plant growing naturally in the substrate.

In time, the front righthand side of the display will be covered by a lush green carpet of *Glossostigma elatinoides*. Three of these low-growing, round-leaved plants will fill the gaps between the specimen plants. We are leaving plenty of space between them for growth, but this invasive species will need controlling.

Together, the four plants should create an interesting foreground, allowing the fish plenty of swimming room, but also providing cover should they require it.

**Below:** *Make a hole in the substrate and plant the* Hygrophila *in the usual way. Pull up the substrate around the base of the plant. This is the view from the front of the tank.*

## Planting Glossostigma elatinoides

**1** To the right of the foreground there are three Glossostigma elatinoides. Given sufficient light, these will make a dense carpet across the substrate, filling in any gaps.

**2** Plant the three Glossostigma, leaving room for them to spread. In time, the plants will merge together to create a seamless carpet of plants at the front of the aquarium.

**Left:** Next to the Hygrophila, the foreground display continues with two plants of Hemianthus micranthemoides that in time will form a bushy clump.

**Right:** In the wild, liverwort forms cushions on stones. For aquarium use, you can buy it already attached to a clay stone that you simply place on the substrate, but can move later on if necessary. As it grows, it will entirely cover the stone.

## THE PLANTED AQUARIUM

Hygrophila polysperma
"Rosanervig"

Echinodorus
cordifolius ssp. fluitans

Hemianthus
micranthemoides

**Above:** As you put plants in the tank, take a look at it from various angles. If the sides are visible, make sure there is some planting of interest there. This view from the righthand side of the tank lends a whole new perspective.

**Right:** The larger species of Echinodorus are very effective for the background of the aquarium, and this "Red Flame" makes a striking focal point. For the best results, provide a nutrient-rich substrate, good lighting and regular iron fertilization.

### Room for development

Do not be tempted to fill the aquarium with plants right away. Allowing the existing plants to spread on their own will always look more natural. If gaps remain, you can always add more plants later on

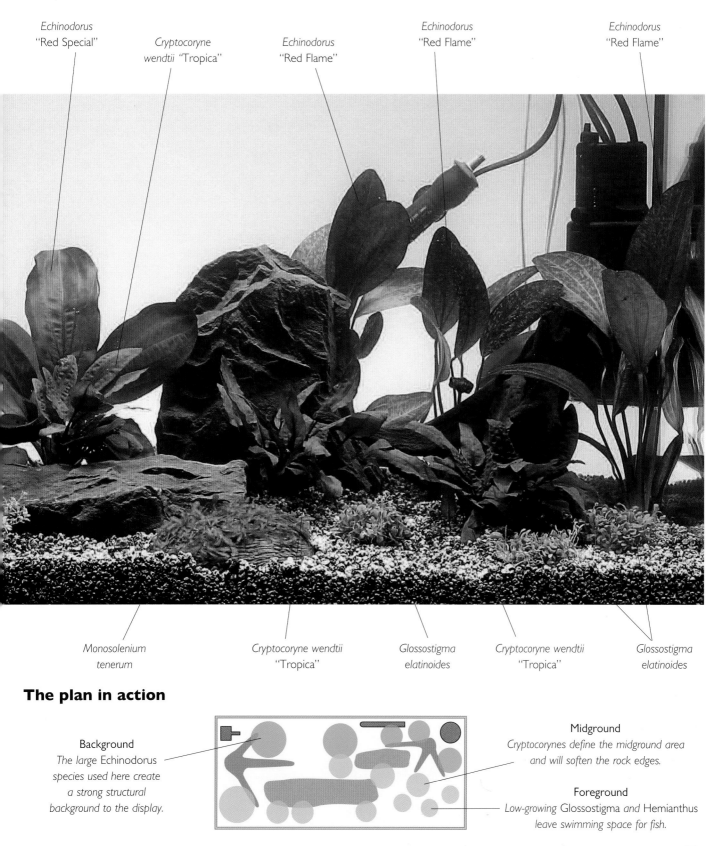

*Echinodorus*
"Red Special"

*Cryptocoryne
wendtii* "Tropica"

*Echinodorus*
"Red Flame"

*Echinodorus*
"Red Flame"

*Echinodorus*
"Red Flame"

*Monosolenium
tenerum*

*Cryptocoryne wendtii*
"Tropica"

*Glossostigma
elatinoides*

*Cryptocoryne wendtii*
"Tropica"

*Glossostigma
elatinoides*

## The plan in action

**Background**
*The large Echinodorus
species used here create
a strong structural
background to the display.*

**Midground**
*Cryptocorynes define the midground area
and will soften the rock edges.*

**Foreground**
*Low-growing Glossostigma and Hemianthus
leave swimming space for fish.*

# PLANT PROFILES

This part of the book features a selection of aquarium plants that will thrive in most conditions. They are grouped according to the main planting zones available within the aquarium display.

**The background** should be dominated by the tallest species, ideally growing up to the water surface. They can vary in appearance, from the ribbonlike leaves of the *Vallisneria* species to the spade-shaped leaves of the Amazon swords (*Echinodorus* spp.). For a subtle change, consider some of the *Hygrophila* species; their mass of small leaves creates a bush effect at the back of the aquarium. As well as leaf type, do not forget to make use of leaf color. You can blend similar foliage tones into a background "curtain" or use contrasting colors for impact.

**The midground** plants form the heart of the display and probably encompass the widest choice of suitable species. They should grow to about half the height of the aquarium, allowing you to view the background plants behind and create the tiered effect that looks so natural. Space out the midground plants a little to leave swimming space for the fish in the center, yet provide sufficient cover for the most timid species. Positioning plants between items of hard landscaping conveys the impression that they are slowly invading the gaps. They will soon fill out,

softening the edges of rocks and bogwood and lending the display a more natural feel. Certain species of plants, including *Anubias* and *Microsorium*, do not grow in the substrate but on porous material, such as bogwood or suitable rock. These plants are ideal for the midground, as they combine hard decor with soft planting. The midground is also the ideal spot for a specimen plant, such as the Madagascan lace leaf plant (*Aponogeton madagascariensis*), that can become a centerpiece of the display.

**The foreground** should feature low-growing species that form a green carpet at the front of the display. *Glossostigma elatinoides* is an excellent example. Most of these species are rampant growers once established and will need regular pruning to keep them under control. It is safest to restrict yourself to one or two species to ensure that you do not end up with a tangle of different plants in the foreground. They will help to frame what is behind and achieve a natural look to the planted aquarium.

**Floating plants** add a finishing touch to complete the underwater scene. Many have trailing roots that provide welcome shade and refuge for timid fish within the aquarium. Floating plants can spread rapidly across the surface and need protection from bright lights that may scorch their leaves.

## Background plants

### *Bacopa caroliniana* ❯
Giant Bacopa

When planted in groups, giant bacopa, from Central America, brings a delicate elegance to the back of the display, where the dense, small-leaved foliage easily hides any unsightly equipment. It can be propagated by cuttings planted around an existing group to increase its size. To thrive, the plant needs good lighting, a fine substrate and a regular supply of nutrients, as well as $CO_2$ fertilization. In good conditions, it can grow to 20–40 cm (8–16 in).

## *Cabomba caroliniana* ▶
### Green Cabomba

Probably the most common of the cabombas, this variety from Central and South America brings a lush, salad-green accent to the aquarium display. The fine bushy growth contrasts well with larger-leaved plants in the midground. Do not plant the stems in a bunch, but separate them out to allow light to reach the base of the plant. Most cabombas will produce sideshoots that can be nipped off with a pair of sharp scissors and replanted around the aquarium to make your cabomba display larger. *C. caroliniana* can grow up to 50 cm (20 in) and fills out the back of the aquarium.

## *Cabomba aquatica* ▲
### Yellow Cabomba

The delicate leaves of this popular and commonly available plant from Central America add a feathery texture to the display. The leaf stalks are equally spaced along the stem, except near the tips, where the young growth is dense. Cabomba is often sold in bunches secured with a lead weight. Be sure to undo the weight and separate the stems before planting them 6 cm (2.4 in) apart, otherwise the lower leaves will not receive enough light and die off. This causes the lower stem to die back, break away and float around the aquarium. Cabomba requires regular feeding and strong lighting to keep the growth healthy and compact. Reaches up to 40 cm (16 in).

## *Cabomba piauhyensis* ▲
### Red Cabomba

Although not entirely red, this cabomba sports a wonderful mixture of flame color shades from red to the lime-green of the new growth. It is usually the case that the most stunning plant needs the most care, and this is also true of Red Cabomba. To provide a stunning backdrop up to 40 cm (16 in) high, it needs excellent $CO_2$ fertilization, very bright light and a regular supply of nutrients. Algae growth will quickly choke the delicate leaves, so make sure that it never gains a foothold. *C. piauhyensis* from Central and South America offers a challenge to the experienced aquarist; beginners should opt for the green variety, which is much easier to keep.

### *Crinum thaianum* ▶
Onion Plant

This stunning species has a very unusual appearance for an aquarium plant. The large, onion-shaped bulb sits half in the substrate, while ribbonlike leaves grow up toward the water surface. Once they get there, and this can even happen in a 1 m (39 in) deep aquarium, they grow out along the surface. You will need to cut back some of these long leaves, as they may reduce light to other plants beneath them. However, it is important not to remove too many otherwise you will spoil the essential "fountainlike" effect of the plant, which also provides valuable cover for the fish. Even though the onion plant is a background subject, choose a spot where at least some of the magnificent bulb can be seen.

### ◀ *Gymnocoronis spilanthoides*
Spadeleaf Plant

This is another plant whose arrangement of relatively small leaves can create a wonderful backdrop for the display. Pairs of leaves grow from a central stem at 90° to the pair below to maximize the light absorbed by the plant. The spade-shaped green leaves can form very quickly; in ideal conditions, *G. spilanthoides* can reach 50–60 cm (20–24 in) and needs regular pruning to prevent it becoming too rampant. If bought in bunches, separate each of the stems before planting so that light can reach the lower leaves.

Hygrophila polysperma *"Big Leaf"* grows larger than the standard form of this hardy plant.

### ◀ *Hygrophila polysperma*
Dwarf Hygrophila

Dwarf hygrophila, from India, is the most commonly available *Hygrophila* species and ideal for the beginner, as its rapid growth and dense foliage reassure the newcomer that things can develop quickly in the aquarium. Regular pruning helps to generate new growth and keeps the plant healthy. As it is such a popular plant, cultivars such as "Rosenervig" have been introduced. The white veins in its leaves add a structural dimension to the plant's appearance. The leaves also turn an attractive pink shade as they reach bright light toward the surface.

### *Hygrophila difformis* ▼
Water Wisteria

This broad plant from India, Thailand and Malaysia has delicate, finely branched leaves that billow elegantly in the flow of water from a filter. To give of its best it needs regular feeding, good lighting and sufficient space. If it is too crowded, the lower part of the plant cannot receive enough light and quickly disintegrates. It will grow to a height of 50 cm (20 in) and is ideal for masking unsightly aquarium equipment.

### *Hygrophila guianensis* ▼
Hygrophila

The large leaves of *H. guianensis* add an unusual shape to the display. Try several stems growing together to make a wall of foliage, 25 cm (10 in) high. However, it is the most difficult species to keep in an aquarium environment, as it needs plenty of nutrients at the roots and strong lighting for its leaves to do well. Beginners will find the *polysperma* species much easier to keep.

### Ludwigia glandulosa
Red Ludwigia

This lush plant from the southern United States is ideal background material. Red ludwigia freely produces oval-shaped pink through green leaves on quick-growing stems, reaching a height of 20–30 cm (8–12 in). As it grows rapidly, you can take cuttings to increase the diameter of the plant group and quickly fill out the display. Leave sufficient space between the stems to allow light to reach the lower leaves. Regular iron-rich fertilization will promote the leaf color and keep the plant in good condition.

### Limnophila aquatica ▲
Giant Ambulia

It would not be difficult to confuse giant ambulia, from India and Sri Lanka, with the Central American green cabomba. Both are fine-leaved bushy plants that grow rapidly; giant ambulia can reach 50 cm (20 in). Its featherlike leaves grow in rosettes from the central stem. Once it reaches the surface, take a single cutting from each stem and replant it to enlarge the group. Allow the cut stems to recover fully before repeating the process. Regular dosing with a multipurpose fertilizer will ensure the plant stays in good health. Like most fine-leaved plants, it will suffer badly if algae is allowed to establish.

### Myriophyllum aquaticum
Brazilian Milfoil

Milfoil could be described as the feather boa of the aquarium plant portfolio. It can add a wonderful fluid texture to the background of the display, as its many fine leaves often completely hide the stems. This fine foliage can also be the plant's downfall, however, as it will trap any passing debris. Efficient mechanical filtration is essential. Keep the plant healthy with regular feeds and strong lighting. Resist the temptation to take stem cuttings; wait until the plant produces a sideshoot and prune this to expand the area of your plant. This South American species can grow to 50 cm (20 in).

## ❮ *Myriophyllum tuberculatum*
### Red Milfoil

The dense, auburn foliage of the red milfoil from Brazil, adds unique color and makes it an understandably popular choice. Strong lighting and regular, iron-rich fertilization are essential for the plant to thrive. In good conditions it can reach a height of 40 cm (16 in). Any debris that circulates around the display will become caught in the leaves, blocking the tiny pores and impeding photosynthesis, so be sure to provide good mechanical filtration to remove even the finest particles. If the plant is sold in bunches, separate out the stems as you plant them to allow light to reach the lower leaves. Only use sideshoots for propagation.

## ▼ *Rotala macrandra*
### Giant Red Rotala

Ruffles of leaves ranging in color from pink to deep red, with a hint of green on the upper sides, make this Indian plant a superb addition to the aquarium. However, as you might expect from a plant with mostly red foliage, only strong lighting and iron-rich fertilization will keep the colors bold on new and existing growth. Furthermore, it is delicate and should be handled very gently, as both the leaves and stems can be easily damaged. The lower leaves can die off if they have insufficient light, so leave space between the stems when planting. In good conditions, giant red rotala can grow to 50 cm (20 in).

## *Nesaea crassicaulis* ▼

This very striking plant for the rear of the aquarium has pairs of lush green leaves growing on strong stems to a height of 40–50 cm (16–20 in). The tips of the new growth are often pinkish; good lighting and regular, iron-rich fertilization will enhance this attractive coloration. The plant holds its elongated leaves horizontally from the stem to gather the most light, and this tendency gives the plant a very strong structural appearance. When planting, leave sufficient space between the stems to allow light to reach the base. *N. crassicaulis* prefers slightly soft water. If you are not certain you can provide the conditions this West African plant requires, then *Hygrophila polysperma* might be a safer option.

### ◀ *Sagittaria subulata*
#### Needle Sagittaria

An ideal plant for the beginner, the needle sagittaria from the eastern United States will grow in most aquarium conditions, reaching a height of 30 cm (12 in). Its long, thin leaves grow in dense bundles to fill out the background. It will thrive in good light, although in deeper-than-average aquariums it may do better in the midground. Needle sagittaria produces runners that spread out to form a curtain of plants that can be used as a "divider" between other plants if your design requires it.

### ▼ *Shinnersia rivularis*
#### Mexican Oakleaf

As the common name implies, this plant's leaves resemble those of the terrestrial oak tree. They grow on tall stems that become leggy in poor light, so provide very good illumination to maintain a bushy shape. Regularly pruning the top growth prevents the development of large leaves that will cut out light to other plants below. Mexican oakleaf can grow up to 60 cm (24 in); to increase the display, prune and replant the side growths.

Sagittaria and Vallisneria are ideal for new aquariums. Their fast growth will mop up any excess nutrients before algae can develop.

## Vallisneria asiatica ▼ var. biwaensis
### Corkscrew Vallis

Growing to a height of 35 cm (14 in), the tightly twisted leaves of this striking plant from Japan make a stunning backdrop in the aquarium. Corkscrew vallis spreads rapidly by means of daughter plants produced on runners and will need controlling to ensure that it does not become too invasive. Do not confuse this species with its smaller cousin, Vallisneria tortifolia, whose leaves are not as twisted and which does not grow as tall.

## ◀ Vallisneria gigantea
### Giant Vallis

If a bold backdrop is what you are after, then the giant vallis from New Guinea is the plant you need. The vigorous ribbonlike leaves, up to 1m (39 in) tall, soon reach the surface and spread horizontally. Careful management will prevent the plant from becoming dominant. As the plant is so vigorous, it requires strong lighting and good-quality, iron-rich fertilization. Yellowing of the leaves is a sure sign that there is an insufficient supply of light and iron. Giant vallis spreads via daughter plants on runners and thrives in cool, moderately hard water.

## Vallisneria spiralis ▶
### Straight Vallis

At 60 cm (24 in), straight vallis is shorter than the giant species and suitable for most aquarium displays. Once the thin, ribbonlike leaves reach the surface, they grow outward to make the best use of the available light. Propagation is via runners from the main plant, and these may need controlling to prevent the plant becoming invasive. In common with most Vallisneria species, established plants send up twisted flower spikes that open just above the water surface. Good lighting and iron-rich fertilization are essential for this plant to thrive.

Vallisneria spiralis "Tiger" has thinner, even more elegant leaves than the natural form.

# Midground plants

### *Ammannia gracilis* ❯
Delicate Ammannia

Ammannia is a very graceful plant from Africa, with thin ribbonlike leaves on a cylindrical stem. Both the leaves and the stem are the same reddish color. As the upper growth can cut out light to the base of the plant, always grow it behind some bushy foreground plants to hide the lower parts. When planted in a group, ammannia can create a very pleasing forest effect. Under ideal conditions it can grow to 50 cm (20 in), but 25–30 cm (10–12 in) is more realistic. Provide plenty of iron-rich substrate and bright lighting.

### ❮ *Alternanthera reineckii*
A plant of colorful contrasts is what you will find with alternanthera. The upper surface of the leaves is olive green, while the underside is a striking pink. The leaf pairs grow from a central red stem. Planting A. *reineckii* in bushy groups creates a more natural effect than planting single stems. An iron-rich substrate will help to enhance the red coloration of this South American specimen, while bright lighting will encourage the plant to grow strongly. Its maximum height in optimum conditions is 50 cm (20 in).

## Anubias barteri ▼

This *Anubias* species from West Africa introduces broad leaves to the midground of the aquarium. The chunky leaves grow from a central rhizome that must be placed above the substrate, otherwise it will rot. Ideally, attach it to a rock or a piece of bogwood. The rhizome will root into the cracks, holding itself firmly in position. Like most aquatic plants, it thrives under bright lighting, but it will readily grow up to 30 cm (12 in) in most aquarium conditions.

## ◀ Aponogeton boivinianus

Usually planted in the midground, this superb species will become the focal point in any aquarium. The long, broad, crinkled leaves are produced from a bulb that contains the plant's store of nutrients. The uneven surface of each leaf provides a huge area through which the plant can soak up the strong light it needs to thrive. If you buy just a bulb then be patient; it will sprout leaves after a couple of weeks. Like most aponogetons kept in good conditions, the plant will produce a flower spike. It may regress into a rest period, much as it would during the dry season in its natural habitat in Madagascar. However, in ideal conditions, most plants will start regrowing after a dormant month or two, attaining a maximum height of 40 cm (16 in).

## Aponogeton crispus ▶

Crinkled Aponogeton

This is one of the most commonly available *Aponogeton* species. In good lighting, it will rapidly produce wavy leaves up to 20–35 cm (10–14 in) long. The structure of the plant is quite loose, and if the light source is poor it will grow to search out more light. Good fertilization is necessary to keep the plant healthy. In ideal conditions, *Aponogeton crispus* will flower in the aquarium. Do not be surprised if after several months of good growth the rate slows down. The plant is not unwell; it is merely resting, as it would during the dry season in its natural Sri Lankan home.

61

### Aponogeton ulvaceus ❯
Wavy Aponogeton

This graceful plant from Sri Lanka has pale green leaves that turn a shade of yellow-orange as they mature. Poor lighting will result in a stunted plant; for strong growth, be sure to provide bright lighting. As with other aponogetons, *A. ulvaceus* will develop in cycles of vigorous growth followed by a rest period. Its maximum height is usually 35–40 cm (14–16 in).

### Aponogeton madagascariensis ▼
Lace Leaf Plant

The unique leaves of this elegant plant create a stunning centerpiece in the aquarium. However, it is not an easy plant to care for and you should seriously consider its requirements before buying it. The skeleton structure of each leaf is made up of interconnecting veins. Good mechanical filtration and regular maintenance are essential to ensure that the water is kept very clean at all times; debris trapped in the leaves is very difficult to remove. In order to thrive, the plant also requires soft water with a pH of 7 or less. A good height for a lace leaf plant in the aquarium would be 35–40 cm (14–16 in).

*Lace leaf plant needs a period of drying out.*

### *Barclaya longifolia* ▶
Orchid Lily

Often bought as a dour-looking corm, *Barclaya longifolia* will reward you with a wondrous display of brightly colored young leaves that become darker green on top and red-brown beneath. The slender arching leaf stalks add a different shape to the display. As the plant grows from a corm, it needs to replace the nutrients it uses up, so provide good fertilization, especially $CO_2$. If you can also supply good-quality bright lighting, *Barclaya longifolia*, from East Africa, is well worth considering as a show plant for the midground. It will grow to 35 cm (14 in).

### ◀ *Blyxa japonica*
Japanese Rush

This Asian plant is difficult to care for, but in ideal conditions it can form a dense mass of leaves. To give it a prolonged, successful life, provide soft water with a low pH, bright lighting and high levels of $CO_2$ fertilization. Although it only grows to a maximum height of 8 cm (3.2 in), the ribbonlike leaves will create a bush effect in the center of the display.

### Cryptocoryne balansae ▼

C. balansae from Thailand is a very different-looking member of the Cryptocoryne group. The ribbonlike leaves with a crinkled, indented appearance contrast well with other plants and add a different texture to the display. The plant grows well in most conditions, but bright lighting will bring out the best in it. The leaves can grow 40 cm (16 in) tall in ideal conditions, but 10 cm (4 in) is the more likely aquarium height.

### Cryptocoryne ▼ pontederiifolia

This is one of the hardiest Cryptocoryne species and an easy plant to grow. Given bright lighting and $CO_2$ fertilization, it will grow up to 25 cm (10 in) high with a similar width. The bold leaf shape of this plant from Sumatra and Borneo will create a central focal point in the aquarium.

### Cryptocoryne cordata ▲

Giant Cryptocoryne

The large oval leaves of this distinctive cryptocoryne from Thailand are an unusual color for an aquarium plant, being reddish-brown on top and dark red beneath. In the right conditions, the leaves can grow up to 15 cm (6 in) long and 6 cm (2.4 in) wide, hence the description "giant" in the plant's common name. To generate these large leaves, the plant requires a good nutrient supply from both $CO_2$ and a nutrient-rich substrate.

## Cryptocoryne undulata ▲
### Undulate Cryptocoryne
Dark-green undulating leaves held on contrasting red-brown leaf stalks are features of this popular midground plant from India. The leaves can reach 30–35 cm (12–14 in) long, but poor light levels will cause it to produce smaller, pale green leaves. Good lighting plus a nutrient-rich substrate will encourage strong growth.

## Echinodorus cordifolius ▶
### Radicans Swordplant
The almost circular leaves of this distinctive plant from North America and Mexico add yet another dimension to a planted display. Single leaves are borne on a succession of leaf stalks up to 40 cm (16 in) tall. Removing older leaves will keep the plant tidy and encourage new growth. Again, this swordplant requires a good supply of iron-rich fertilizer for healthy growth. The plant produces a flower spike that unfurls to reveal small white flowers above the water level.

## ◀ Echinodorus bleheri
### Broadleaved Amazon Swordplant
This easy-care plant from South America is probably the most common Amazon Swordplant found in aquarium shops. When planting, leave plenty of space around it for future growth, and place undemanding foreground plants in front to hide the base, which can look messy with age. The vigorous growth needs to be fuelled by bright lighting and a constant supply of iron-rich fertilizers, plus $CO_2$. In ideal conditions, this plant will reach 50 cm (20 in) high and produce flower spikes and runners that enable it to spread around the aquarium.

*Large leaves with strong veins make a bold statement in the aquarium display.*

## ❮ *Echinodorus macrophyllus*

Large-leaved Amazon Swordplant

Since this statuesque Amazon swordplant from Guyana and Brazil can reach 50 cm (20 in) tall and produce leaves 20 cm (8 in) long, it is really only suitable for the most spacious aquariums. The large oval leaves will block out light to other plants, although regular pruning should keep the plant in check. As there are so many swordplants to choose from, however, a smaller species would be a better option for medium-sized aquariums.

## ❮ *Echinodorus major*

Ruffled Amazon Swordplant

The elongated leaves of *E. major* are ruffled around the edges. To thrive, the plant requires iron-rich fertilization and bright lighting. This Brazilian plant, which can grow to 50 cm (20 in), is ideally suited to the larger aquarium, where it makes an excellent centerpiece.

## *Echinodorus osiris* ❯

Red Amazon Swordplant

In *E. osiris*, one of the most stunning Amazon swordplants, the young red leaves revert to the more traditional green as they mature. Another notable feature of this species from Brazil is the clearly visible structure of veins in the leaves. In common with the other swordplants, it requires bright lighting and iron-rich fertilization to reach its maximum height of 40–50 cm (16–20 in).

## Echinodorus "Red Flame" ❯

This is another cultivated variety that is popular with aquarium plant growers. The stunning green-and-red mottled leaves produce a striking display and add variety to any aquarium. The red speckled effect is evident throughout the life of each leaf. The plant, originally from South America, will grow up to 40 cm (16 in) tall, making it an ideal focal point in the aquarium.

## Echinodorus palaefolius var. ❯ latifolius

The oval green leaves of this specimen swordplant from Brazil are borne on stalks that can be 30–35 cm (12–14 in) tall. Its vigorous growth rate, however, ensures that new leaves are constantly emerging to cover up the base of the stalks. Give this plant plenty of room and avoid placing light-dependent species under its generous canopy. Bright light and iron-rich fertilizers will maximize its potential, although it will grow in most conditions.

## ▼ Echinodorus parviflorus

As one of the more compact species of Amazon swordplant, E. parviflorus from South America is ideal for most aquariums. The short leaf stalks carry compact leaves that are elongated to a pointed tip. Used in the midground, it will hide the unsightly stalks of taller plants at the back of the aquarium. Provide the usual high-iron fertilization and bright lighting to ensure that the plant reaches its potential mature height of 25 cm (10 in).

67

### Echinodorus "Rubin" ❯

The leaves of E. "Rubin," one of the most stunning cultivated hybrids available for aquarium keepers, vary in color from red to green as the plant grows. The leaf veins are very visible, making this cultivar an excellent focal point in the center of the aquarium. The mature leaves have a tendency to spread as opposed to growing up toward the light, so give the plant plenty of room. Bright lighting and iron-rich fertilizers will keep it in good health. It can grow to 50 cm (20 in).

*Boldly marked leaves in shades of red and green make this plant a stunner.*

### Echinodorus uruguayensis ▼

Uruguay Amazon Swordplant

With numerous thin leaves measuring up to 30 cm (12 in) long, this swordplant from Southern Brazil and Uruguay is an interesting departure from the usual broadleaved species. As it grows, it creates a fan effect that looks excellent in the midground. When young, the leaves are often reddish in color, making a wonderful contrast with the adult green leaves. Bright lighting and an iron-rich, fine substrate will keep the plant in good condition. It can tolerate slightly cooler water conditions than other swordplants.

### Echinodorus "Red Special" ▼

The name of this cultivated swordplant variety clearly explains its appeal. The copper-red foliage is markedly different to the usual green swordplant species and makes a great addition to any aquarium. The large, oval leaves often spread out, so give them plenty of room when planting. Bright lighting, iron-rich fertilizer and the addition of $CO_2$ all help to ensure that the plant looks its best and remains the 40 cm (16 in)-tall showpiece of your aquarium display.

### ◀ *Heteranthera zosterifolia*

Stargrass

Borne on thin stems, the leaves of *H. zosterifolia* from Brazil are produced in a starlike arrangement. The plant's main requirement is good lighting and given this it will remain compact, forming dense bushy growth up to 40–50 cm (16–20 in) high in the middle of the aquarium. A lack of light will cause it to grow to the surface in search of more illumination. Once it has found a level with sufficient light, it will throw out more sideshoots and become bushier. Stargrass provides an excellent contrast to larger-leaved plants.

**Above:** *The branching stems of* Hydrocotyle leucocephala *add a vertical accent to this display.*

### ◀ *Hydrocotyle leucocephala*

Brazilian Pennywort

With circular leaves measuring 3–5 cm (1.2–2 in) across, pennywort makes a distinctive addition to the aquarium. It is a fast grower, up to 50–60 cm (20–24 in) tall, and needs regular pruning to keep it under control and prevent it smothering other plants. Bright light is the most important requirement. The shoots double as runners; if they break off, they will readily form new plants.

### Ludwigia arcuata

The dense growth of this *Ludwigia* species from North America makes it ideal for the midground of the aquarium. The leaves are narrower still than those of *L. repens* and the plant can make a pleasing contrast when placed next to its cousin. The leaves require strong lighting and iron-rich fertilization to develop a reddish hue. In low light, the leaves will stay a pale green and the plant will not thrive. To maintain the dense appearance, trim off any leggy growth.

### Microsorium ▶ pteropus "Tropica"

In this cultivated variety of Java fern, the deeply cut leaf edges appear to form lobes. The plant's requirements are the same as for normal Java fern.

### Ludwigia repens

Narrow-leaved Ludwigia

In its different forms, this small-leaved plant from Central and North America brings a variety of leaf shapes and color to the aquarium. In *L. repens*, the leaves are dark green to brown on top, with a reddish-green underside. Being a fast-growing plant, it will quickly make an impact in the aquarium. As it grows, the plant produces pairs of leaves along the stem. At each junction between a leaf and the stem a bud develops that can grow to form an entirely new shoot with its own set of leaves. The gaps between the leaves are governed by the amount of light the plant receives; the greater the light intensity, the closer the leaf pairs are together. It can reach a height of 50 cm (20 in) and may need controlling to stay in scale with other midground plants.

## *Microsorium pteropus* ❯
### Java Fern

This is one of the easiest plants to keep in the aquarium. In its natural environment in Southeast Asia, it grows both submerged and above water on rocks and wood at the edge of streams and rivers. If sold unattached, be sure to tie it to a rock or a piece of bogwood, using cotton or thin fishing line. Older leaves often have plantlets growing on them and these can be used for propagation. In nature, they form new plants that fall from the parent plant as the old leaves die off. *M. pteropus* will grow slowly to 25 cm (10 in) and form a bushy plant. It will thrive in a wide range of aquarium conditions and does not need bright light.

## *Microsorium pteropus* ▼ "Windeløv"

An even more finely cut edge gives the tip of each leaf of this variety a feathery appearance. In addition, the leaves of this highly sought-after aquarium plant are generally more compact than those of the normal Java fern, making it suitable for the smaller aquarium.

## *Nymphaea stellata* ❯
### Red and Blue Water Lily

Being a smaller-leaved species than *N. lotus*, this water lily from India is a better choice for the more compact aquarium. The leaves are not mottled, but range from brownish pink to red. Removing long-stemmed leaves helps to keep the plant compact. Plant the bulb with the crown showing; if buried too deeply, it has a tendency to rot and die off.

**Above:** *The leaves of* Nymphaea lotus *"Zenkeri" vary in color and pattern between specimens.*

### ❮ *Nymphaea lotus*

Tiger Lotus

Water lilies are popular the world over and this East African species is ideal for the aquarium keeper. All water lilies like to grow to the surface to gain maximum benefit from the available light, but this is not always desirable in the aquarium. Removing any leaves that look as though they will reach the surface — and this can happen in as little as three to four days — will encourage the plant to produce more submerged growth. The mottled green-and-red leaves can reach 18–20 cm (7–8 in) across, producing a bold aquarium display. Give *N. lotus* plenty of room in the middle of the aquarium so that it does not cut out light to other plants. All the leaves grow from a tuber, which should be planted in the substrate with just the top of the crown showing.

## Sagittaria platyphylla ▼
### Giant Sagittaria

Although S. platyphylla can be grown as a foreground plant, it often reaches 20 cm (8 in) tall, so is better suited to the midground. The word "Giant" in the common name refers to the broad leaves that grow in a fan shape and make a bold contrast with other plants across the middle of the display. To thrive and spread, S. platyphylla requires regular iron-rich fertilization as well as bright, good-quality lighting.

## ▼ Vallisneria americana
### Jungle Vallis

Vallis americana is ideal for planting at the sides of the midground area. Here, the ribbonlike leaves that twist as they grow to 50–100 cm (20–40 in) will effectively hide any aquarium equipment. This North American plant spreads by producing runners and the daughter plants will form a dense patch under ideal conditions. Given bright light, it will also produce flower shoots that wind their way to the surface and bear a small white flower.

**Above:** The slender leaves of Vallisneria americana catch the light in this display.

## ◀ Rotala rotundifolia
### Dwarf Rotala

In contrast with most midground subjects, this small-leaved plant from Southeast Asia makes an ideal bushy group when several specimens are planted together. The leaves and stem are a lush green color; in good light, the leaves may acquire a pinkish hue toward the tips. In addition to good-quality bright lighting, a regular supply of nutrients will help it thrive.

73

## Foreground plants

### *Anubias barteri var. nana* ❯
Dwarf Anubias

This is probably the most popular *Anubias* species. It is also one of the smallest and lends itself beautifully to planting at the front of the display. The *nana* variety, from West Africa, has waxy round leaves on short stems that grow from the creeping rhizome. The plant's stocky appearance seems to deter the unwanted attentions of herbivorous fish. This undemanding species grows slowly to a height of 12 cm (4.7 in) and can be bought growing over a rock or a piece of bogwood, which adds extra interest to the display. Other anubias include *A. barteri var. caladiifolia*, *A. b. var.* Petite, *A. coffeefolia* and *A. gracilis*.

### *Anubias angustifolia* "Afzelii" ▼
Narrow-leaved Anubias

*Anubias* species are among the most robust and undemanding plants you can add to your display. They grow from a rhizome and produce plenty of leaves. "Afzelii," from West Africa, has crisp, green, pointed leaves that form a tough, bushy plant generally ignored by fish. It is best positioned at the side of the foreground area as it can reach 20 cm (8 in) tall, although this could take some time. If it becomes a little big for the foreground, move it back slightly to blend with the midground plants. Like other *Anubias* species, it can be attached to rocks or bogwood. This excellent starter plant for the aquarium will thrive with $CO_2$ fertilization.

### ◀ *Bacopa monnieri*
Dwarf Bacopa

With regular pruning and in good-quality, bright light, dwarf bacopa will develop into a compact, bushy foreground plant less than 10 cm (4 in) high. It produces small clusters of thick, oval leaves. However, in low-light aquarium conditions, growth will be long and leggy, with larger spaces between the leaves. Keep the shoots trimmed to maintain a low-lying habit.

### *Cryptocoryne albida* ▼

The slender leaves of this beautiful cryptocoryne can vary in color from green to reddish brown, and contrast well with other foreground plants. To create a display with visual impact, plant it in a group of at least three. C. albida, from Thailand, requires regular fertilization and bright, good-quality light if it is to remain compact. In poor light, growth will be leggy. Like all cryptocorynes, it appreciates a substrate augmented with laterite and in the long term will benefit from fertilizer tablets close to its roots. It will reach 25–30 cm (10–12 in) in height.

### ◀ *Cladophora aegagropila*
Moss Balls

These slow-growing spherical balls of algae add a hugely original and interesting plant form to the foreground. Buoyed up by gases released during photosynthesis and respiration, they float to the surface, then sink again when the gases are released.

### ◀ Cryptocoryne willisii

This tiny Sri Lankan cryptocoryne, which only grows to 5 cm (2 in), is another ideal foreground subject. It has broader leaves than *C. parva* and also spreads to fill a space across the front of an aquarium. Like all small plants, it requires strong lighting but is otherwise easy to care for. Provide regular fertilization to ensure that it remains healthy.

### Cryptocoryne beckettii ▼
Beckett's Cryptocoryne

Although it only grows to a maximum of 15 cm (6 in), this attractive cryptocoryne from Sri Lanka produces large, deep green leaves that complement the reddish-brown stalks. This excellent foreground species looks best when planted in a small group and will bush out in time. Make sure that taller plants behind do not block out the light, otherwise the plants will suffer. Provide a good-quality substrate and add nutrients in the form of root tablet fertilizers. Corydoras and other small fish species enjoy the cover created by the broad leaves.

### ▲ Cryptocoryne parva
Dwarf Cryptocoryne

Once established, this beautiful delicate, thin-leaved cryptocoryne from Sri Lanka creates a "lawn" across the entire front of the aquarium. However, to achieve this effect you will need to provide a nutrient-rich substrate and good-quality, bright lighting.

*C. parva* grows to a maximum height of 5 cm (2 in) and makes an excellent complement to its larger relatives.

### Didiplis diandra ❯

This North American species likes to grow toward the surface to a height of 25–35 cm (10–14 in) and therefore may seem an unusual inclusion as a foreground plant. However, it can be kept smaller with regular pruning to make it produce bushier sideshoots and a hedgelike appearance. Its delicate, feathery leaves help it stand out from most other aquatic plants. In good lighting, the uppermost leaves change color from green to rusty brown. It requires bright light, soft water and regular feeding with iron-rich food. If any long tips of growth break off, simply push them into the substrate.

### Cryptocoryne walkeri ❯

Being a slightly taller cryptocoryne, *C. walkeri* makes an excellent side foreground plant to soften the corners of the aquarium. It is one of the most commonly available species and its dark green leaves with brown undersides are popular with aquarium keepers. When planted together with a carpet of *C. parva*, it can create a complete foreground. *C. walkeri*, from Sri Lanka, grows up to 12 cm (4.7 in) high and looks best planted in a small group. It is easy to grow and will benefit from regular fertilization.

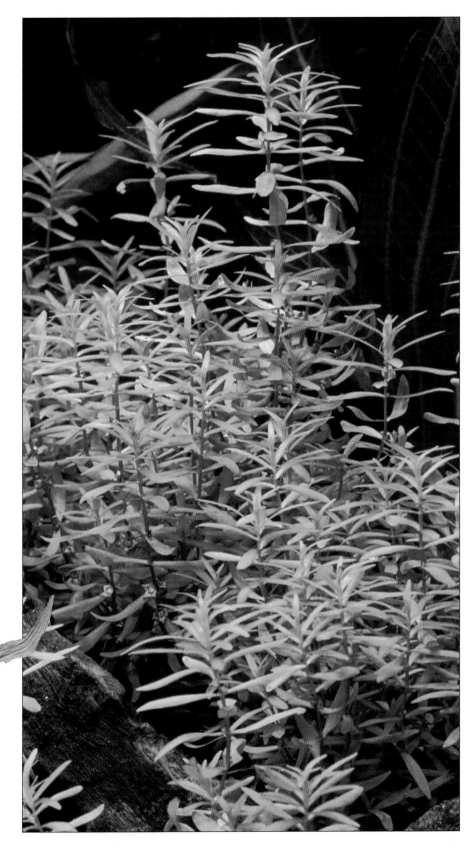

### Echinodorus tenellus
Pygmy Chain Swordplant
Originating from North and South America, this is one of the most popular foreground plants but requires good conditions if it is to thrive. In bright lighting and given a fine substrate, it will spread to form a carpet only 8 cm (3.2 in) high across the front of the display. Any lobe-shaped leaves on a newly acquired plant are an indication that it has been grown above water. However, these leaves will die back once the plant is submerged, to be replaced by thinner, aquatic foliage. If the plant becomes too invasive, simply cut off the runners and lift out the unwanted pieces.

### Eleocharis acicularis ❯
Hairgrass
This grasslike aquatic plant is readily available from most aquatic stores. In dim conditions it will grow leggy, but under bright light and with regular doses of fertilizer, it bushes outward, creating an interesting texture in the display. Be sure to include some corydoras catfish in the aquarium to eat or dislodge any debris that becomes trapped in its fine leaves. If these become clogged, the plant may die back. Can grow to 25 cm (10 in), but usually 15–20 cm (6–8 in).

### *Fontinalis antipyretica* ▶
Willow Moss

This interesting small plant from North America, Europe, Asia and North Africa makes a distinctive addition to the display. It produces numerous, small, sail-like leaves 0.5 cm (0.2 in) long on thin stems and attaches itself by its roots to rocks and bogwood. Happier in cooler conditions, it enjoys moving water from the filter outflow. When you first buy willow moss, handle it gently and anchor it carefully to a piece of wood or rock in the foreground using fine fishing line. In bright light, it will spread to create a mat that covers the line and rapidly looks as though it has always grown there.

### ◀ *Eusteralis stellata*
Star rotala

Although this stunning plant from Australia and Asia can grow to 40 cm (16 in) tall, regular pruning and the correct conditions can keep it squat and bushy, making it an excellent foreground subject. To keep the starlike rings of foliage looking their best, provide strong lighting, high levels of dissolved carbon dioxide and a substrate rich in nutrients. Although the star rotala makes high demands, it rewards in equal measures.

### *Glossostigma elatinoides* ▼

Originating from Australia and New Zealand, *Glossostigma* must be the ultimate foreground carpet plant. Providing it receives strong lighting and $CO_2$ fertilization, it will form a dense mat across the entire foreground area, softening any hard edges and corners. The effect is of a display that has been cut out of a river bed. It rarely grows more than 1.5 cm (0.6 in) high. If the plant is growing healthily, you can often observe how the small, lobed leaves trap escaping oxygen produced during photosynthesis. Arrange the plants in small groups to start with and watch as they blend into one mass as they become established.

79

### *Hemianthus micranthemoides* ❯
Pearlweed

At 15–20 cm (6–8 in), *H. micranthemoides* from Cuba and southeastern United States is slightly taller than dwarf helzine, and can be kept bushy with regular trimming. Try to keep it free of debris, as the fine, lobed leaves easily become clogged with suspended particles. To create a carpet effect you will need several individual plants, but these will soon blend together to give the impression of a single, larger plant. It is vital to provide bright, good-quality lighting.

### *Hydrocotyle sibthorpioides* ▼
Dwarf Pennywort

Borne on low-growing runners, the round leaves of this *Hydrocotyle* species introduce a different foliage shape to the foreground. This Southeast Asian plant requires bright light if it is to do well, but in the right conditions will grow reasonably quickly to cover the substrate. For maximum effect, plant a group of three or more. It will reach 12 cm (4.7 in) high.

### *Hemianthus callitrichoides* ▼
Dwarf Helzine

This compact Central American plant creates a dense mat of small round leaves 3–15 cm (1.2–6 in) high. It has neither the growth rate nor the marauding tendencies of *Glossostigma*. Dwarf helzine can form an excellent contrast to other foreground plants, such as the smaller cryptocorynes. All *Hemianthus* species require a good supply of nutrients and bright lighting, without which they soon suffer and die off.

▼

## *Micranthemum* ▶ *umbrosum*

Helzine

Unlike *Glossostigma*, which grows in an organized manner, *M. umbrosum* provides a jumbled display of foliage in the foreground. It is an attractive, squat plant from Central America that produces copious amounts of very small, round leaves on cresslike stems up to 30 cm (12 in) tall. In bright light, it remains more compact. It can grow as a floating plant, but may need regular cropping to prevent it shading the aquarium below.

## *Lilaeopsis mauritiana* ▼

Grassplant

This tufty little plant from the Indian Ocean island of Mauritius spreads across the foreground, complementing the broader-leaved plants behind and providing cover for smaller fish. Corydoras catfish provide a useful service by keeping it clear of debris. Strong lighting and a fine substrate will ensure healthy growth. The plant grows 5–10 cm (2–4 in) tall, but regular trimming will keep it under control. Cutting it back to different heights will result in a more natural look.

## *Monosolenium tenerum* ▼

Pellia

Originating from Asia, this stunning, small-leaved, fernlike plant is sold attached to rocks or purpose-made "plant stones." In good lighting and with reasonable $CO_2$ fertilization, this "living fossil" soon creates a pad of foliage in which fish love to rummage. *Monosolenium* does not have true leaves, but grows thalli, which look like webbed pads that fork as they grow. Small pieces break off, lodge elsewhere in the aquarium and start new plants. This unusual species can be tiered toward the back of the aquarium to create an impressive display.

# Floating plants

### *Pistia stratiotes* ❯
Water Lettuce

This excellent floating plant is best suited to the large aquarium. It produces velvety, lettucelike leaves above the surface and long, feathery roots below. The plant absorbs nutrients through the roots, which also provide welcome shade and sanctuary for fish. Good ventilation above the aquarium is required if the plants are to do well, but otherwise it is easy to care for.

### *Limnobium laevigatum* ❯
Amazon Frogbit

Resembling mini lily pads, these chunky, small, round-leaved plants from Brazil float around the aquarium in the flow of water. They can easily spread to cover a large area of the tank, so be prepared to keep them under control. Daughter plants produced on runners soon provide a clump of leaves under which surface-dwelling fish can hide.

### *Riccia fluitans* ❯
Crystalwort

Unusual, but hardy and undemanding, this simple floating plant spreads by division of the growing tips. Careful management may be required if it becomes too vigorous, as it will cut out light to the plants beneath it. It is a very adaptable plant that will do well in most aquariums.

## ◀ *Salvinia natans*
Salvinia
The leaves of this *Salvinia* species from Europe, Asia and North Africa have a crinkled appearance, which helps to distinguish it from *S. auriculata*. Like all floating plants, it provides excellent cover for surface-swimming fish.
The feathery roots extract nutrients from the water; good fertilization will help the plant stay healthy.

In *Salvinia oblongifolia* (inset) the leaves are more oval and elongated, but the plant's requirements are similar to those of other *Salvinia* species.

## *Salvinia auriculata* ▶
Salvinia
This fast-growing plant from Central and South America produces pairs of velvety leaves above the water surface as it drifts around the aquarium. It grows by absorbing dissolved nutrients from the water through its roots. In time, it can create a dense carpet across the surface, so make sure it does not get out of control and block out all the light to the plants below. Without sufficient ventilation above the tank, bright halide lighting may scorch the leaves.

# LIGHTING

All life on our planet ultimately relies on light energy from the sun to survive. Plants use sunlight for photosynthesis to build simple sugars as the starting point of all food chains. In the "artificial" environment of the aquarium, the lighting system must perform the roles of providing light energy for plants to flourish and to illuminate the display so that fish can feel at home and we can see and enjoy the combined result.

## What is light?

Visible light occupies a relatively narrow band in a wide span of electromagnetic energy that stretches from low-energy radio waves at one end to high-energy gamma waves at the other. The only difference between these forms of energy is their wavelength, commonly measured in nanometers (nm) — billionths of a meter. The visible light spectrum starts at infrared (700 nm) and extends to ultraviolet (400 nm). Between these are the rainbow colors we are familiar with, ranging from red and orange through yellow to green and blue. Combined, they make white light.

This explanation might seem rather scientific, but it is important to understand how light works so we can choose the most efficient lighting system for the aquarium display.

## What light do plants need?

Most plants use the green pigment chlorophyll to trap sunlight for photosynthesis. Chlorophyll absorbs mainly red and blue light. (It makes plants look green simply because it reflects and does not absorb green light.) In the red part of the spectrum, the wavelengths between 650 nm and 680 nm are the most efficiently trapped by chlorophyll.

Land plants receive equal shares of all the wavelengths of light from the sun. However, submerged aquatic plants must cope with the light filtering effects of water. The longer wavelengths at the red

## Recreating natural light in the aquarium

**Left:** *In some parts of the Amazon River Basin the water is crystal clear and the strong tropical sunlight supports a rich growth of aquatic plants. The right kind and intensity of lighting will help you to recreate this luxuriant growth in your display aquarium.*

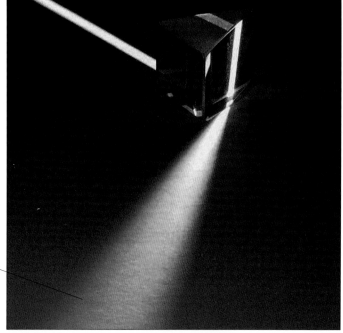

**Right:** *Shine a beam of white light into a glass prism and, amazingly, it emerges as a mini rainbow. The prism is revealing the spectrum of colors that make up white light. Understanding how nature uses these colors is the key to successful lighting.*

*The visible spectrum ranges from violet, through blue, green, yellow, orange and red.*

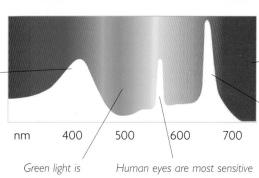

*Sunlight peaks in the blue area of the spectrum. This short-wave light is used by both plants and algae.*

*Light in the infrared area (700–750 nm) cannot be used by plants*

nm  400  500  600  700

*Green light is reflected by the majority of plants.*

*Human eyes are most sensitive to yellow. Aquarium lights should include a peak here.*

*Aquatic plants' photosynthetic ability is most sensitive to red light between 650 and 680 nm.*

# Shifting the natural light cycle

## The tropical day

*The typical tropical day is lit for about 12 hours from 7 am to 7 pm.*

| 0 | 2 | 4 | 6 | 8 | 10 | 12 | 14 | 16 | 18 | 20 | 22 | 24 |

## The aquarium day

*Shifting that 12-hour period to 11 am to 11 pm provides an evening viewing period.*

| 0 | 2 | 4 | 6 | 8 | 10 | 12 | 14 | 16 | 18 | 20 | 22 | 24 |

**Above:** *The lighting system in our featured aquarium has one triphosphor white tube and one "pink" tube to enhance plant growth.*

end of the spectrum are less active and are quickly absorbed, whereas the shorter blue wavelengths are more energetic and penetrate deeper into the water before being absorbed. (This explains why undersea views in tropical diving films look so blue.) To compensate for this unequal absorption, the light source for aquarium plants should have a high peak in the red band around 650 nm and also a significant peak in the blue part of the spectrum. For us to see the display, there should also be a peak in the yellow band, because human eyes are most sensitive to this part of the spectrum.

## Choosing aquarium lights

Commonly used aquarium light sources fall into three categories: fluorescent tubes, light-emitting diodes (LED) and metal halide (halogen) lamps.

**Standard fluorescent tubes** are a familiar part of our domestic and working environment. They are glass tubes coated on the inside with phosphors that glow (fluoresce) when bombarded with high-energy electrons. The starter (ballast) unit triggers the process. The wavelengths of light produced depend on the phosphors in the coating. For a balanced output in the aquarium, choose a fluorescent tube with the three required peaks of blue, red and yellow. These are best produced

by triphosphor tubes — each of the three phosphors generating a different wavelength of light. For a good level of illumination, use two or more tubes above the aquarium, but this depends on how much room there is inside the hood.

Fluorescent tubes are very cheap to buy and run. A 75 cm (30 in) tank only needs two 25-watt tubes to illuminate it. One drawback with using fluorescent tubes, however, is that they radiate in all directions and bounce light around the hood instead of down into the aquarium. This can be resolved by fitting an inexpensive reflector that directs the maximum amount of light downward. Another drawback of standard fluorescent tubes is that their low power consumption limits their capacity to produce light bright enough for aquariums deeper than 45 cm (18 in). Because of this, standard tubes are increasingly being replaced with T5 tubes.

**T5 high-output tubes** are thinner than standard fluorescents, or "T8" tubes, but produce around 50% more light, so they are a much better option for planted aquariums. T5s are more expensive than standard T8 tubes, but are becoming the aquarium standard in lighting. The range of different tubes available offer varying spectrums of light. Conveniently, you only need to read the packaging to find

which is most suitable for growing plants. Arguably, a disadvantage with all tubes is that they are designed to give uniform light: whereas other lights can give a sparkling effect.

**Other types of tube** include single-ended tubes, where the tube is bent in two with the fitting at one end. These types of light are particularly useful for small tanks, where full-length tubes may be difficult to fit into a small hood. The quality of output for these types of light varies considerably, so make sure they are specifically designed for aquarium use. Some small tanks also have "screw-in" type bulbs that closely resemble energy-saving household bulbs. These will provide good illumination, but may not produce an ideal spectrum of light. If you want the best for your plants it is worth shopping around.

**Metal halide lamps** are the best choice for aquariums that are 50 cm (20 in) or deeper, and if your plants require very bright light. These units are much more expensive than other lighting, both to buy and to run, but nothing comes close to the brightness and spectrum of the light produced, with power ratings of 70 watts per lamp. The lamps are cased in reflectors that direct all the light down into the tank, so it is very directional and creates a dramatic effect of strong shadows. The disadvantage of metal halide lamps, aside from their cost, is that they run very hot and therefore must be suspended over an open-topped tank. This allows the lights to remain cool and avoids over-heating the aquarium, but it does mean that there will be increased evaporation from the water surface that may cause unwanted condensation elsewhere in the room. Some designs allow the lamps to hang on a bracket that is attached to the aquarium or its stand, others require fixing to walls or ceilings. Despite their excellent light output, the problems associated with metal halide lamps means that increasingly they are being replaced by light-emitting diodes (LEDs).

## Light-emitting diodes (LED)

LEDs combine all of the best features of aquarium lighting in one package: they are very cheap and efficient to run (typically one watt per bulb); they can be designed to produce a huge range of light colors; they are very long lasting (10 years) and

**Above:** *The familiar fluorescent tubes used across the world in homes and offices are fine for aquarium use. The development of a triphosphor coating has boosted the output across a wide range of light wavelengths.*

**Above:** *A narrow-bore form of fluorescent tube provides intense light and saves space in the aquarium canopy. These are triggered with an electronic starter (ballast) system and are available in a range phosphor types.*

**Above:** *Good quality, high-output LED lighting systems such as these are expensive but very bright, and may eventually replace most forms of aquarium lighting.*

**Right:** *This 20 cm LED light fitting is ideal for a child's aquarium. It is a low-voltage unit and so safe to fit and use. It can be easily installed into the lid of any small tank.*

**Above:** *Twin tubes, such as this biax tube, occupy a smaller space than two single tubes and produce a more intense light. Each side can be manufactured with a different light color.*

## Waterproof lights and covers

Most aquariums fitted with fluorescent tubes will have waterproof end caps protecting the tube fittings and do not need protective covers or condensation trays to prevent water splashing or condensing on the tubes. However, some light units may not have such protection and are instead enclosed in a plastic cover screwed into the hood. When choosing your tank it is worth noting that these plastic covers often degrade with time and become opaque rather than clear, reducing the amount of light reaching the aquarium. With typical use, the cover may need replacing every few years, so make sure the aquarium is a known brand so that you can be sure that you will be able to obtain the right replacement covers easily for the life of the aquarium.

*Right:* Limescale from splashing water, algae deposits and minor damage to covers will reduce the amount of light reaching the water.

produce intense light with very little heat.

Aquarium LED lighting is a relatively new technology and to begin with the units were prohibitively expensive. However, with widening demand, manufacture and competition, prices are now much more reasonable, particularly when the additional savings of bulb replacements and running efficiency are taken into consideration. LEDs are sold in units consisting of groups of bulbs arranged either in a row or a square block, which will suit any shape of aquarium and lighting requirement. They can be fitted under a hood or suspended above the tank and will provide a bright, sparkling effect in the water.

*Below:* A simple way of boosting light levels reaching the aquarium is to fit a reflector around the fluorescent tubes in the hood.

*Below:* Metal-halide lamps for aquarium use are fitted into housings such as this and suspended above the open tank. They provide very bright illumination, but must have ventilation space around them because of the heat they generate.

## Use aquarium fittings

Always use lighting equipment specifically designed for use with aquariums, both from a safety and an efficiency standpoint. Light sources that are not designed for aquarium use will not supply the specialist needs of aquarium plants and may not be suitable for safe operation close to water.

## Installing the lighting system

**Right:** *Our featured aquarium has a lighting cradle that accepts two conventional fluorescent tubes and fits snugly into the frame over the tank.*

*This rigid aluminum cradle will provide years of safe, corrosion-free service.*

**Above:** *Slip the locking collars onto each tube and align the pins correctly before sliding them into the sockets at both ends of the lighting cradle.*

**Above:** *Carefully tighten up the locking collars at each end to secure the tubes in place. These will make a waterproof seal around the endcaps.*

**Left:** *A view looking down into the aquarium shows the lighting cradle in place, complete with the fluorescent tubes. The cradle is part of an aluminum frame that fits over the top of the tank.*

*The starter (ballast) system for the tubes is housed in the central section of the cradle.*

## Conventional fittings

The long-established lighting method involves fitting fluorescent tubes into the hood with flying leads connecting them to the starter (ballast) system.

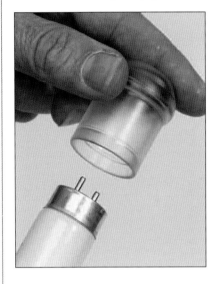

**Above:** *To protect tubes from moisture over the aquarium, waterproof endcaps are fitted on the flying leads. Align the pins to the socket and push the tube firmly but carefully into each endcap.*

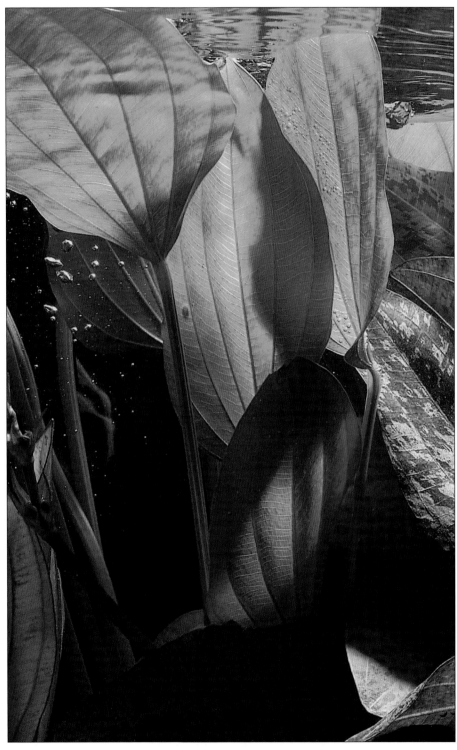

**Above:** *From an aquarium plant's point of view, the lighting system is the tropical sky — complete with a substitute sun providing the sole source of illumination. Plants vary in their demands for light. The aquarium may seem brightly lit to our eyes, but it may be too dark for some plants to thrive.*

# WATER CHEMISTRY

Our aquarium is on the verge of becoming a miniature version of a real aquatic environment. There is a layer of fertile substrate that will nourish the aquatic plants through their first few months of life. There are rocks and pieces of bogwood to give fish shelter and security. There are lights to simulate the radiant energy of the sun. The water is warm and flowing through a filter system matched to the size of the tank. Only the fish are missing. But before we add them it is vital to consider the water. More so than with any other pet, fish are reliant on their keepers for the upkeep of their whole environment, right down to the oxygen they breathe. Fish are generally very hardy, but any deterioration or sudden variation in the quality of the water they inhabit will affect them profoundly. It has been said that keeping fish is mostly a matter of keeping water: fish will look after themselves.

Understanding how to keep water quality in top shape is not difficult, but it does require a grasp of the characteristics and components of water, the impact that fish have on it, and how this impact is managed by us.

**Above:** *Tap water is processed for human consumption. The chemicals added to it by the water company make it safe for us to drink but dangerous for aquarium fish. Treat it before use.*

## Making tap water safe for fish

Tap water is the most convenient source of water and is used by the majority of fishkeepers across the world. However, tap water is supplied to our homes fit for human consumption. To achieve this, water companies treat the supply with chemicals such as chlorine and chloramine (a combination of chlorine and ammonia) to kill harmful bacteria. Even at their low dosage rate, these harsh chemicals pose real problems for aquarium fish, principally because they damage the delicate skin and gill membranes.

It is a golden rule, therefore, that all tap water should be conditioned before use, not only when the aquarium is filled for the first time but also during water changes carried out as part of routine maintenance. Used as recommended, liquid tap water conditioners will neutralize chlorine and chloramine and also deal with any heavy metals that the water has picked up during its journey to your home. The most advanced products also contain an aloe vera colloid to provide a protective layer in addition to the fishes' own mucus coating and add beneficial bacteria to boost the natural biological cycles that keep the water clean in a well-balanced system.

Because of their substantial volume, large aquariums (over 2 m/6.5 ft long) will need a great deal of water conditioning. In this case, one option is to invest in a reverse osmosis (RO) water purifier. These units contain a semi-permeable membrane that effectively strains out everything dissolved in the water at a molecular level. In fact, the resulting water is so pure that minerals must be added to make it appropriate for fish. RO units are expensive and the filter cartridges need occasional replacement. Also, up to 85% of the water they take in is lost as waste rather than produced as purified water. If buying an RO unit does not make economic sense, you can buy supplies of RO water from aquatic retailers.

**Above:** *Treating tap water with a conditioner is a simple process. Following the maker's instructions, add the required amount of conditioner to tap water in a bucket before use in the tank.*

**Below:** *A reverse osmosis unit will filter out suspended particles and remove all dissolved substances at the molecular level. RO water is so pure it needs added salts for fishkeeping use.*

## What does pH value mean?

The pH value is an indication of whether water is acidic, neutral or alkaline. The scale extends from 0 to 14, with 0 being extremely acidic and 14 extremely alkaline; pH 7 represents the neutral point. It is important to realize that the pH scale is logarithmic, with each unit reflecting a tenfold difference. Therefore, pH 6 is ten times more acidic than pH 7 and 100 times more acidic than pH 8.

The pH of natural water supplies can be "shaped" by various influences, including the amount of pollution in the air through which rain falls, the surface soil on which it lands and the underlying rock over which it flows. Once inside the aquarium, other factors continually affect the pH of water, such as biological filtration and the respiration of plants and fish.

It is essential to check the initial pH of water intended for the aquarium and to continue checking it in order to maintain a uniform pH value. Fortunately, it is easy to determine the pH value of water by using a test kit, which can be a dip strip, tablet or liquid test kit. Whichever method

## The pH scale

*The two elements (hydrogen and oxygen) that make up water exist as positively charged hydrogen ions ($H^+$) and negatively charged hydroxyl ions ($OH^-$). The pH scale reflects the relative amounts of these two ions. Water with more hydrogen ions than hydroxyl ions is acidic, whereas a greater number of hydroxyl ions makes the water alkaline. Water with equal numbers is neutral.*

pH 9

pH 8

pH 7

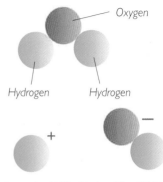

Water molecule ($H_2O$)

Oxygen

Hydrogen          Hydrogen

+          −

Hydrogen ion ($H^+$)   Hydroxyl ion ($OH^-$)

*The pH scale is logarithmic, meaning that each unit change in pH, say from 7 to 8, is a ten times change; from 7 to 9 is a hundred times change, and from 7 to 10 reflects a thousand times change. This is why sudden changes are stressful to fish.*

## Contrasting pH values

The natural environments of commonly kept aquarium fish can differ quite markedly in the pH value of their native waters. Discus (*Symphysodon discus*) live in acidic Amazon tributaries in South America at pH 6, whereas cichlids in Lake Tanganyika in eastern

Africa thrive in alkaline water at pH 8–8.5. Since the water of the Amazon environment is one hundred times more acidic than in Lake Tanganyika it is not surprising that you never find these two types of fish happily thriving in the same aquarium.

Cyphotilapia frontosa

*Lake Tanganyikan cichlids live in hard, highly alkaline waters.*

*Discus come from areas with soft, acidic water.*

you choose, be sure to pick one that is easy to use and is packed with clear information about the results you get.

A good aquatic retailer will be able to tell you whether your local water supply is suitable for the species of fish you wish to keep or whether it is necessary to adjust the pH value in order for the fish to thrive in your system.

Changing the pH value of your aquarium water is quite an undertaking. Once you commit to a specific pH and the fish that require it, every water change will have to be adjusted appropriately. Also, pH is very closely related to the "hardness" of the water so they cannot be managed separately. It is easy to change the pH of water with very few minerals (and ironically rather difficult to keep it stable), but water with lots of minerals will resist any attempts to change its pH. In fact, after the pH of hard water has been changed it will

often slowly revert to near previous levels. Nevertheless, if pH does have to be changed there are a number of products that will achieve it. Bottles of pH adjuster available from your aquatic retailer will work very quickly on the water. Alternatively, there are natural products, such as peat, bogwood and Indian almond (Catappa) leaves, to lower the pH (make it more acidic) through the release of tannins. These tannins will also turn the water golden/amber, even darker brown over prolonged periods, which may not be to your taste. To raise the pH, use rocks containing calcium such as limestone. Whatever method you choose, change the pH very gradually and monitor it continually. For all these reasons, many people prefer to obtain the fish and plants that suit their local tap water, particularly when starting out, and your local aquarium shop will be happy to advise you of those.

## Hard and soft water

As the rock over which water runs helps to determine its pH value, it also influences its hardness. Water hardness is a measure of the dissolved minerals it carries, mainly carbonates and sulphates of calcium and magnesium. Water with a high salt content is referred to as hard, while water low in these minerals is referred to as soft.

The total (or general) water hardness value is measured in degrees of hardness (°dH) and can be divided into two types: temporary hardness, which can be removed by boiling the water; and permanent hardness, which cannot. Test kits are available for both total and temporary hardness. The scale for total hardness ranges from 0°dH (very soft) to 28°dH and over (very hard).

It is possible to change the hardness of water, but it should be done gradually, with an understanding of the implications this will have on other water quality

## The nitrogen cycle

*Your aquarium is a miniature version of the natural world. Powered by bacteria, the nitrogen cycle converts nitrogen-rich wastes into a series of successively less poisonous substances.*

*Nitrates are readily taken up by plants as a food source, usefully reducing the levels in the tank.*

*Nitrobacter bacteria convert nitrite to nitrate ($NO_3$), which is much less harmful to the aquarium fish.*

*After digesting nitrogen-rich foods (such as protein), fish excrete extremely toxic ammonia ($NH_3$) directly from the gills and also in urine and feces. Decomposing biological matter, such as uneaten food and dead leaves, add to the ammonia load in the aquarium.*

*Bacteria, such as Nitrosomonas, in the biological filter (and also coating surfaces within the aquarium) convert ammonia to nitrite ($NO_2$), which is still dangerous, even at low concentrations.*

## Upsetting the nitrogen cycle

Chemical treatments added to the aquarium may reduce the level of nitrifying bacteria in your filter. Always monitor the water quality during and after their use to ensure that no undue stress is placed on the fish.

Household cleaners used near the aquarium can cause a bacterial "wipeout" in the filter. Be careful using furniture polish or glass cleaners near the tank and never use them on the hood, where the risk of contamination is at its greatest.

If you detect an unexplained rise in ammonia and nitrite, check the aquarium carefully for dead fish and/or uneaten food as these can cause a dramatic deterioration in water quality.

## Free and ionized ammonia

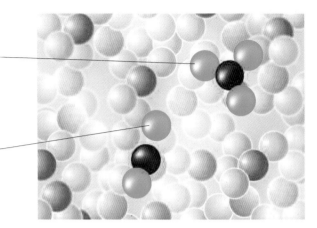

*Free ammonia ($NH_3$) consists of one atom of nitrogen and three of hydrogen.*

*The nitrogen atom of ammonia attracts a hydrogen atom from water ($H_2O$).*

*The hydrogen atom attaches to the nitrogen atom, conferring a positive charge on the newly created ammonium ion ($NH_4^+$).*

*Without one hydrogen atom, the water molecule becomes a negatively charged hydroxyl ion ($OH^-$).*

variables such as pH. Bear in mind that whatever water hardness you adjust to, you will have to maintain it permanently. Increasing the water hardness is relatively straightforward: anything with calcium (such as limestone) will help, or there are specific products that can be added to the water to increase the level of minerals safely and effectively. Softening water can be done by using RO water (see page 90), or water softening resins that are a cheaper alternative to RO. Alternatively, you may dilute the hard water with rainwater, which has no hardness at all since it has never run over the rocks that add minerals. Unfortunately, rainwater can also carry pollution, particularly in highly urban areas. If you are in any doubt, filter the rainwater through carbon.

As an aquarium matures, processes such as the nitrogen cycle remove the water hardness and lower the pH, so it should be routinely checked using test kits. The harder the water, the more slowly this change will take place.

In most natural environments, the pH value and hardness are linked, with low pH water being soft and high pH water being hard. The hardness of your aquarium water will also give you an indication of how stable the pH is likely to be. In soft water, the low level of dissolved mineral salts provides less resistance (buffering capacity) to changes in pH, which tends to drop. Hard water has a greater mineral content and is said to have a high buffering capacity, and so the pH remains more stable.

Fish and plants prefer differing hardness values if they are to thrive. Broadly speaking, most plants prefer slightly softer water because the $CO_2$ is more available there. However, your local aquatic retailer will be familiar with the local water conditions and will be happy to guide you toward fish species suited to them or advise you on changing your water hardness and/or pH

if you have your heart set on a particular type of fish that requires anything different.

## The nitrogen cycle

Understanding the nitrogen cycle is the single most important aspect of successful fishkeeping. It is a natural process that occurs in every aquatic habitat around the world. The key compounds in the cycle all contain nitrogen ($N_2$), which makes up 80% of the air we breathe and on its own is a harmless inert gas. Combined with hydrogen, however, nitrogen makes ammonia ($NH_3$), an extremely poisonous substance. Even at very low concentrations, it will rapidly kill all the fish in your aquarium. This is a convenient, if dramatic, point to break into the nitrogen cycle and trace how ammonia is converted into progressively less toxic compounds until the cycle starts all over again.

## Life can poison itself

All plants and animals in the natural world respire, using oxygen to release energy from food (which includes nitrogen-rich amino acids and proteins) and produce organic waste. Plants produce organic waste relatively slowly through the gradual decomposition of their leaves and stems. Aquarium fish produce organic waste much more rapidly, actively excreting ammonia from their gills as a direct byproduct of respiration. They also produce organic waste in the form of small amounts of urine and also solid feces. All this waste forms free ammonia in the water — potentially a self-poisoning situation for the creatures living in it.

## Bacteria to the rescue

Of course, nature would not allow life to poison itself. As in all natural cycles, what is waste for one set of creatures becomes food for another. The rescue party in the aquarium (and all aquatic habitats) is led by bacteria that consume the ammonia and use oxygen to convert it into nitrite

($NO_2$) — a process called nitrification. For many years these aerobic (oxygen-loving) bacteria were thought to be a type called Nitrosomonas. However, it is now understood that there is a range of different species that vary from place to place, so they are collectively called ammonia-oxidizing bacteria (AOB). The bad news is that although nitrite is less toxic than ammonia, it is still deadly in minute quantities. Fortunately, a second set of aerobic bacteria, once called nitrobacter but now collectively termed nitrite-oxidizing bacteria (NOB), use oxygen to convert nitrite into nitrate ($NO_3$), which is not nearly as toxic.

## The cycle turns

The production of nitrate provides the impetus to keep the cycle turning. Nitrate is used by plants as food for growth and the nitrogen it contains becomes incorporated into the amino acids and proteins that make up the structure of leaves and stems. When the plants die and decompose or are eaten by fish, the

waste produced releases ammonia into the water and the nitrogen cycle takes another turn.

## How toxic is toxic?

Free ammonia ($NH_3$) is extremely toxic, easily passing from the bloodstream into the tissues and brain and causing damage and behavioral impairment. Levels over 0.02 ppm (parts per million) or 0.02 mg/l are poisonous to fish. For any given amount of ammonia in the water, the proportion in the free form rises as the temperature and/or pH value increase. In cooler more acidic water, more of the ammonia is in the less harmful ionized form ($NH_4^+$). A golden rule for successful fishkeeping is a zero reading for ammonia levels.

Nitrite combines with the oxygen-carrying pigment hemoglobin in the fish's blood, preventing the red blood cells from picking up oxygen. (Affected blood turns from a healthy red to a damaged brown color.) A classic sign of nitrite poisoning is fish gasping at the surface. This is not a lack

**Left:** When taking a water sample, select a clean test vial and rinse it in water taken from the aquarium. Washing it in tap water may distort the final test results.

**Below:** Tests usually involve starting with a water sample of 5 or 10 ml. For accurate results, make sure the water surface level sits on the line printed on the vial.

## Keeping a record

During the first few weeks of setting up the aquarium it is worth keeping a note of the date and the results of your tests. This could be invaluable information should you have problems in the future that you want to discuss with your retailer.

**Above:** Adding the right amount reagent is also vital. Invert bottles for standard-sized drops. Tablets contain a measured dose.

## pH test

The pH test indicates how acid or alkaline the water is. Tests are available to provide broad-range (shown here) and narrow-range readings. It is a good idea to continue testing the pH throughout the life of the aquarium because ongoing processes such as biological filtration will affect the pH value of the water over time.

## Water hardness test

Hardness test kits should be able to register both temporary and total hardness to give you the full picture of your water chemistry. Most are simple color change kits in which the number of drops required to change the color of a sample indicates the degrees of hardness.

## Dip tests

Dip tests consist of paper or plastic strips with impregnated pads that change color when the strip is dipped briefly in a water sample. Comparing the color change against a printed reference chart provides readings of several parameters. While one-off tests are a good introduction to water testing they are not the best option for long-term use as the risk of contamination of the test strips is quite high.

*Above:* Dip the test strip directly into the aquarium.

*Right:* Compare the color with the printed chart. This test shows a water hardness of 14°dH.

## Ammonia, Nitrite, Nitrate

When testing for any of these substances it is best to carry out tests for all of them because this will reveal the complete biological status of the aquarium. If you simply test for ammonia and you are happy that you record a zero reading, you will probably have a high level of nitrite and your fish will be suffering. Once the first fish are added you should test the water every day until both ammonia and nitrite are under control. Then repeat the tests weekly to ensure that the biological balance of the aquarium is continued with the addition of any new fish. Repeat the tests for a week whenever new fish are added to the aquarium.

*Right:* This total ammonia test shows a reading of 0.4 mg/l (0.4 ppm). This toxic short-term level will fall as filter bacteria respond.

*Left:* A nitrite result of 0.25 mg/l can be fatal for some fish species and needs to be reduced to zero for safe fishkeeping.

*Right:* Nitrate levels can go quite high, especially in sparsely planted tanks where the plants do use enough of it as food. This 25 mg/l result is typical and safe in most aquariums.

## Phosphate

Testing for phosphate is usually recommended if the aquarium appears to be suffering from an algae problem. Some phosphate may come in with the tap water used to fill the aquarium and is also an ingredient in fish food. If allowed to rise above the level at which the aquarium plants can use it as a fertilizer, the excess will become food for fast-growing algae. A phosphate test is shown in action on page 146.

**Above:** *Carefully measure out the correct amount of filter start-up product needed for your aquarium system. Be sure to allow the precise instructions provided with the product.*

**Right:** *Add the measured amount directly to the aquarium water. These products provide heterotrophic bacteria that will foster the growth of beneficial bacteria to deal with nitrogenous waste.*

## How a biofilter works

NOB *bacteria grow in the foam and convert ammonia into nitrite.*

As levels of nitrite increase, AOB *bacteria convert it into the less toxic nitrate.*

of oxygen in the water, simply that the fish are suffocating as their blood cannot carry enough oxygen. If you see this, always take immediate action to reduce nitrite levels, such as making a water change (see page 150). Lethal nitrite levels differ between fish species, but 0.2 mg/l can be fatally toxic. Again, the only acceptable level in the aquarium is a zero reading.

Nitrate is relatively harmless in comparison to ammonia and nitrite. High nitrate levels can cause health problems for young fish and fry; however, the main problem will come in the form of unwanted algae growing in the aquarium. Nitrate is a major nutrient for plants and any excess will fuel a growth explosion in a wide range of algae species that will rapidly make a mess of your aquarium. It is important to monitor nitrate levels and keep them below 50 mg/l. A healthy population of aquarium plants can keep levels of nitrate below 10 mg/l.

It is always worth testing your tap water for nitrate, since filling the aquarium from the tap will introduce a certain level to your system. This nitrate comes from fertilizers used in agriculture that wash into the water supply chain and are eventually piped to your house.

### How to test water

Controlling the water conditions is the key to a successful aquarium. A vital part of this is to measure, record and compare the values of a number of characteristics that reflect the state of the water circulating around the tank. Here, we look at the practical details of testing water for all the major parameters, from pH to nitrate levels.

### Using test kits properly

The test kits available today are easy to use and provide accurate results. The most popular kits involve adding liquid or tablet reagents to a water sample and comparing a color change to a printed chart. Instant-result dip strip tests are also available for many parameters. Tablet kits are probably the best ones for consistent results because the amount of reagent is provided in a precisely measured dose.

If you are taking a water sample in a

test vial provided in the kit, rinse it first in water taken from the aquarium. Also, when the filling the vial to the desired level (usually 5 ml or 10 ml), check that the bottom of the water surface is on the 5 or 10 ml mark. This will ensure that the test is as accurate as possible. Hold liquid reagent bottles fully inverted to ensure that a uniform drop size is achieved from the dropper. Varying drop sizes will influence the results and not give you an accurate reading.

Once you have finished your tests always wash out and dry your test vials before storing the whole kit in a safe place away from children, as many reagents used in water tests are potentially harmful. Keep test kits out of direct sunlight, not only to keep the chemicals stable but also to prevent color reference charts fading in bright light. Refills are available once you have used all the reagents, which saves you having to buy the entire kit again.

The water tests featured on pages 94–95 are the most important ones used in the aquarium hobby.

## Maturing the filter

As we have seen, the nitrogen cycle is nature's way of dealing with its own waste products. However, in the highly managed aquarium environment we must harness the cleansing power of the nitrogen cycle bacteria effectively so that they can deal with the waste produced by the livestock.

## How your filter works

The nitrifying bacteria that break down nitrogenous waste will coat all surfaces inside the aquarium but not in sufficient numbers to control the amount of waste

*Right:* A healthy aquarium is easily achieved by having the right number of fish and plants and adequate filtration to keep the water quality perfect. Once this balance is achieved, it is important to test the water regularly, as small changes will naturally happen as the fish and plants grow and the aquarium matures. Many of these changes can be counteracted with weekly water changes of 10% of the tank volume.

produced by your fish. This is why we need a biological filter. The filter medium, in our case the blue filter foam, provides a huge surface area in a compact space on which bacteria can grow. Eventually, the bacteria will multiply to fill the filter sponge and control the waste produced by the fish, giving zero readings on ammonia and nitrite test kits. However, nitrifying bacteria are very slow-growing and to build up a population that can process the aquarium wastes might take six to eight weeks, a long time when we want to stock the tank with fish.

In order to curtail this long wait, there are a number of things we can do. Essentially, we need to add pioneering bacteria to start colonizing the filter, and we need to give them enough food with

which to grow. Since the sequence of products (ammonia, nitrite and nitrate) being transformed from one to another is termed the nitrogen cycle, it is fitting that the process by which we can encourage it along is called cycling. There are two main forms of cycling: one that involves adding fish and one that does not. In both processes the same sequence happens, just at different rates. It may take two or three weeks for the filter bacteria populations to develop, which may seem like a long time. Meanwhile you can make any final adjustments to the decor and the plants can grow and establish their root systems. That way, when it is safe to add your fish, the aquarium, the fish, the plants and you are all perfectly happy with it.

## Which method should I use?

The graph shows the general sequence of cycling. The populations and activity of the filter bacteria can be judged by testing the water for the products they process. As the AOB colonize, they convert it to nitrite and therefore the ammonia levels fall at the same rate as nitrite levels rise. Eventually, nitrite levels will similarly fall as it is turned into nitrate by NOB. When the NOB populations have stabilized, the filter is said to be mature, or fully cycled, and the aquarium can be properly stocked. However, the graph is only a guide. Every aquarium is unique, varying in water quality, temperature, substrate and even the planting levels. Ultimately, the end process will be the same: no ammonia, no nitrite; and small (but rising) levels of nitrate but the process of getting there either employs fish or excludes them.

The first method involves adding some hardy fish that will provide ammonia for the filter to start processing. This method is easiest because it relies on the fish continually adding waste for the filter. The types of fish typically used as starter fish are more tolerant of less-than-perfect water quality. However, this method of cycling is becoming less popular, as many people feel uncomfortable adding fish to an environment that is not perfect. Furthermore, these tough fish may not be species you want in the final tank display. In any case, there are fishless alternatives that just require a little bit more time or effort.

## Fishless cycling

Any other freshwater aquarium (such as a friend's) will have billions of the bacteria in the filter and over the substrate. Taking a small amount of old media and "seeding" your aquarium filter with it will kick-start the bacteria colonies. In fact, part of maintaining any aquarium involves washing the mechanical filter (such as wool or sponges), and the resulting dirty water makes a perfect filter starter, having both waste (bacteria "food") and vast numbers of bacteria. It is important to be selective about the aquarium you take bacteria from: it should have no history of disease or snails. As the filter bacteria grow, they will need continual feeding, which can be provided by adding a very small amount of fish food every few days. This will break down, releasing ammonia that will then be fed into the nitrogen cycle. Even the plants you have added will bring in helpful bacteria and provide food through the odd leaf that falls off. If all this seems a little haphazard, manufacturers have developed many products to standardize this process. These contain food and different types of bacteria. They must be added to the tank regularly until it is fully mature — ammonia and nitrites have peaked and fallen to zero.

The products differ in what they contain, how regularly they are applied, and what type of bacterial culture they include. Unlike many types of bacteria, nitrifying bacteria do not have a dormant state; they must be maintained in a thriving culture to survive, which is difficult to achieve in a bottle that might be kept on the retailer's shelf for weeks. Some manufacturers seem to have surmounted the challenge through sophisticated biochemistry and technical advances. These live cultures will sometimes be kept refrigerated at the aquatic store to prolong their life. The best of them are so effective that you can add a few of your first fish within a few days of adding the starter. It is easy to see why such a product would be popular, and new creations are being developed all the time. Your local aquatic retailer will be able to advise you of the full range.

However you decide to cycle your tank, it is important to test ammonia, nitrite and nitrate very regularly and to keep note of their values. It is exciting to see the process develop because you know that the time to add fish is getting nearer.

It is an increasingly common practice to carry out regular water changes while the aquarium is maturing. This might slow the cycling process down a little, but it does help avoid algae blooms. When the aquarium is first set up there are a lot of nutrients in the water because plants have not become established. In addition, ammonia and nitrite themselves act as

*Left:* Adding fish to an aquarium may take months until the tank reaches its maximum stocking capacity. But that gives you plenty of time to consider what your next fish will be!

fertilizers. What can happen is that algae, which are very fast growing, can exploit this brief upsurge in nutrients and rapidly colonize the aquarium. Eventually, as the aquarium matures and water quality stabilizes, the algae will succumb to the dominant plants. To minimize the issue entirely, many people prefer to undertake regular (even daily) water changes of 10-20% of the aquarium volume in the first couple of weeks.

## Troubleshooting ammonia

Ammonia will quickly cause health problems in the smallest doses, but after the aquarium has matured it should not be seen again, because it is continually processed into nitrite. If, when you are doing your normal water testing, you do find ammonia then there are a couple of

things that could have gone wrong. First, there is too much waste. This is usually due to overfeeding or, much more rarely, a fish has died. It might also happen if a large number of fish have been added in at once; the filter just needs a little time to upgrade to the new ammonia production. The other reason for elevated ammonia is that the filter cannot cope with the usual waste levels. This could be due to the bacteria being damaged somehow. For example, a powercut will starve the filter of oxygen and the millions of the bacteria will perish within 20 minutes. Many aquarium treatments can have an impact on filter bacteria. However the filter has been damaged, it just needs time to recover. In effect, you are building up the bacteria populations as though starting from scratch. Of course, until the

### Clear water may be deadly

My water is crystal clear, so it must be OK. Why do I have to use a test kit? Every aquatic retailer has heard this question a million times. The simple answer is that the deadly toxins ammonia and nitrite are invisible. The water may be gin clear but it could be deadly and kill fish in minutes. The only way to be sure is to check the water quality using a test kit. These are simple to use and for a minimal investment can save the lives of the fish and other creatures in your care.

*Below: The sequence of nitrification is always in the same order, but the timing and strength of each "peak" will vary between every aquarium.*

## Cycling the aquarium

**Days 1–5** *Waste in the tank begins to rot, releasing ammonia which, because the AOB population is not yet established, gradually increases in level.*

**Days 5–10** *AOB populations develop, consuming ammonia and converting it to nitrite, which increases as ammonia levels fall.*

**Days 10–18** *As nitrite levels increase, NOB have more "food" and their population grows. With it, the levels of nitrites fall and levels of nitrate climb. When the nitrite levels are continually zero, the filter is mature. Nitrate levels constantly increase because they are the last part of the process, so they need to be removed with regular (weekly) water changes.*

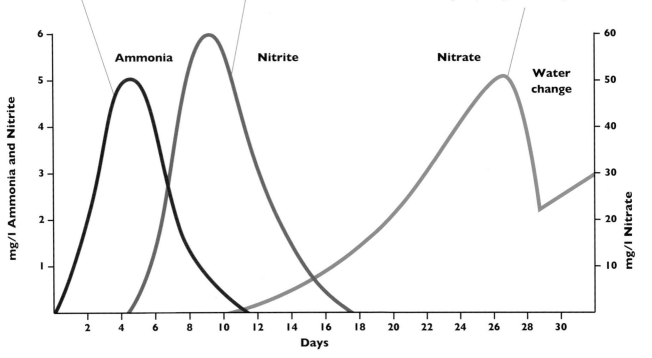

## Ammonia production

All living things need nitrogen to make proteins, which are used to make everything from muscle to hormones. Fish also use protein as an energy source, and when they do the nitrogen is excreted as a waste product. Fish excrete 90% of their total nitrogen waste from their gills, and the majority (over 85%) of this is in the form of ammonia. In large water bodies the ammonia is diluted so much that it effectively disappears, but in the aquarium the volumes of water are relatively small and so ammonia can accumulate to levels that are toxic to the fish. Ammonia is particularly unpleasant because it is damaging in so many ways: it blocks blood from transporting oxygen, it is toxic to cells, it irritates membranes such as on the skin and gills, and it inhibits the fishes' ability to balance their internal salt levels. Because of this multiple toxicity, it is easy to understand why fish are so affected by even the smallest quantities of ammonia. If ever it is found (through water tests), immediate action must be taken to minimize the exposure.

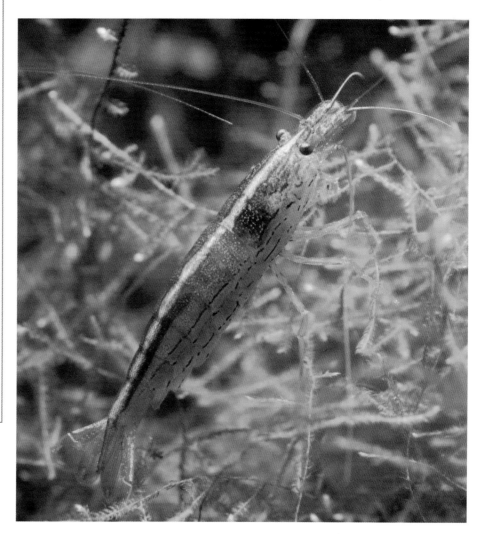

**Below**: The Amano shrimp (Caridina multidentata) is one of several freshwater shrimp species that are becoming very popular in aquaria. They are relatively undemanding in terms of water quality as long as extremes of pH and hardness are avoided. However, they are very sensitive to ammonia and nitrite, so do not introduce them until the aquarium has matured.

bacteria are established there could be poor water quality. Fortunately, there are products that will absorb or neutralize the ammonia very effectively. Of these, the ammonia neutralizers are preferable. The ammonia will still be available for the bacteria to use, but it will not be in a form that is toxic to fish. In the short term, to avoid any damage to an aquarium suffering from ammonia poisoning, just carry out frequent water changes until you are able to obtain the products.

When testing for ammonia, it is vital that the readings are taken with reference to the pH. If the pH is less than 7 (in other words slightly acid), virtually any ammonia in the aquarium is in a much less toxic form called ammonium. Both ammonia and ammonium are so chemically similar

that test kits cannot distinguish between them, so the results of the test kit can at first glance appear very dangerous. That is why they should always be interpreted with reference to pH to identify whether any ammonia is in the very toxic form or not. In any case, the reason for elevated ammonia levels should be investigated and remedied.

## Troubleshooting nitrite

Like ammonia, nitrite should never appear in an established aquarium. If it does,

there are a couple of possible reasons. Any ammonia (caused by overfeeding, a dead fish or damaged filter) will, of course, eventually appear as a nitrite "spike." Previously, we have discussed the different bacteria responsible for removing ammonia and nitrite. Each of these groups have optimum conditions outside of which they will not thrive, and process wastes, as well as they should. NOB are more sensitive to low oxygen levels and lower temperatures (below 25°C/77°F) than AOB. So after a powercut, when the filter

**Above:** *Being moved from the shop to your tank is likely to be one of the most stressful events in your fishes' lives, so take good care and make sure your water conditions are suitable.*

**Above:** *Activated carbon is extremely effective at removing many toxins from the water, but will not remove ammonium, nitrite, nitrate or phosphate. Resins in permeable bags inside the filter can be used to remove a range of chemicals.*

has no oxygenated water passing through it and the heaters are off, the NOB will be hit more than the AOB. As a result, nitrites may accumulate at a rate faster than the NOB can process them. However, as with ammonia, there are a number of products that will absorb excess nitrites. Some are granular or resins, some are liquid. They are very effective and will remove nitrites overnight. In the meantime, water changes will keep danger at bay.

## Troubleshooting nitrates

Nitrates are at the end of the production line. Very little consumes them and they will typically build up. Luckily, they are nowhere near as damaging as ammonia and nitrite. Nevertheless, nitrates are not harmless: high levels will cause stress in fish and cause some types of algae to proliferate. For these reasons, it is best to aim for levels less than 50 mg/l. There are a number of methods of ensuring that this is achieved. Some nitrates will naturally be used up in an aquarium by small colonies of special bacteria that live in oxygen-depleted areas such as deep in the gravel, and plants will also take up nitrates. In some aquariums this is enough to keep levels low, but most aquariums will need a little extra help through the use of chemical filtration media and

regular small water changes. If you still experience rising nitrate levels above 50 mg/l, nitrate-absorbing or reducing treatments are available.

## Troubleshooting pH and water hardness

All processes in an aquarium – the respiration of the fish, bacteria and plants, the nitrogen cycle and the leaching of many types of wood – will make conditions gradually more acid. As acid is produced it is buffered (mopped up) by minerals in the water that contribute to hardness (page 92), but in so doing, the hardness is removed. Because of this, it is possible for both the pH and hardness to suddenly drop without warning. This can be prevented with regular water changes that remove the extra acid and add more hardness to the aquarium. If the worst happens, substantial water changes will eventually bring them both back to normal. However, make sure the water has some hardness; RO or rainwater will not help at all in this instance.

# BRINGING THE AQUARIUM TO LIFE

Three weeks after the initial setting up, the plants are growing and the different areas of the display are starting to blend together. Do not worry if some species do not appear to have developed much; growth rates vary and in time all the plants will flourish as they settle into their new home. To keep the aquarium in pristine condition, clean and without any evidence of algae or other problems, it is important to begin a maintenance regime at this stage. This is a habit you must acquire, but usually only involves carrying out small but regular tasks that are all part of being a successful aquarist and, hopefully, more of a pleasure than a chore.

Be sure to turn off the power supply to the aquarium before putting your arms into the water. If the tank is very full, first remove up to a bucketful of water, otherwise the water will flood, which is both messy and potentially very hazardous. The third week also begins the most exciting aspect of creating your display: bringing the aquarium to life by introducing the first fish. However tempting it may be, do not buy all your fish at once; follow the guidelines set out on page 108.

*With the aquarium planted up at the end of day two (above), it was left to settle. Since then, the plant roots have established and there is clear evidence of growth (right).*

*Plants have given our living picture a framework that will come alive with the addition of some well-chosen fish.*

## TIDYING UP THE TANK

Plant growth is evidence of life in the aquarium, but this means that smaller life forms, namely algae, are also trying to gain a foothold. If you inspect the front glass, you will probably notice the appearance of small green spots, both here and on the rocks and internal equipment. This spot algae can be removed with a wad of filter wool, which is effective even on the most stubborn encrusted algae growths. The algae scraper and the magnetic algae cleaner are more up-to-date tools for this job. In good models of algae scraper, the handle on the scouring pad should be slightly angled to enable you to access the corners of the tank and exert more pressure when required. To use a magnetic algae cleaner, place the magnet faced with the scouring material inside the tank and guide it from outside with the other magnet. The internal magnet has a string attached so that you can retrieve it from the base of the tank if it sinks. Modern magnets with internal air pockets will float if they become detached.

*Above:* An algae magnet enables you to clean the glass inside the aquarium easily without getting your hands wet.

### Trimming plants

Some plants will grow vigorously and may need trimming. The stems of tall plants, such as hygrophila, often grow out in the wrong direction and if left, would ruin the display. These can be simply trimmed back using a pair of sharp scissors. Always cut just above a node — the point where the leaves are attached to the stem — to stimulate new growth from the buds at the base of each leaf. With luck, these will grow out in the right direction.

*Above:* Always use products designed specifically for aquarium use. This algae pad contains no chemicals and will not scratch the glass, unlike some similar-looking household products.

*Right:* Using a scraper on the end of a handle is another method of cleaning the glass. The rough surface deals safely with stubborn marks. Clean glass is a sign of a well-cared-for aquarium.

Some foreground plants can grow quite tall and will need regular trimming to keep them under control. This is the case with the hemianthus in the featured aquarium. The aim is to ensure that it stays bushy and does not grow leggy or obscure the swimming space behind it.

Now is also the time to attend to the larger-leaved plants toward the back of the display. Using scissors, remove any damaged, algae-encrusted or generally spent leaves. Trim these as close to the base of the plant as possible, without damaging any new growth.

**Right:** *The hemianthus in the foreground at the lefthand side of the aquarium has produced some long shoots. To encourage a bushy habit, trim away the excess growth with sharp scissors.*

**Left:** *The hygrophila also needs trimming. Think about where to snip off a long shoot. Cutting just above a node will encourage the plant to produce new, bushy growth.*

**Below:** *This long shoot is growing out sideways and spoiling the appearance of the display, so cut it off. You can replant these trimmings to fill a gap elsewhere.*

## Coping with larger plants

**Left:** When removing foliage from a large-leaved plant such as this echinodorus, cut the stalk at a point near the base. This encourages new leaves to develop and is a good way of maintaining compact growth.

**Below:** Algae is growing on this leaf, so dispose of it. Older, larger leaves generally die back first, which is a shame as these are the ones that make the most impact, initially, but new ones will soon take their place.

**Right:** It is interesting to compare this view of the tank before the glass was cleaned and the plants trimmed, with the view below. If you neglect to monitor and trim the plants, stronger varieties can soon swamp smaller, less vigorous ones.

**Below:** *Do not be afraid to trim back wayward shoots or damaged leaves, even if it means exposing some of the wood, rocks and equipment again. Healthy plants grow back rapidly.*

## ADDING FIRST FISH

With the aquarium up and running reliably and the plants in place, you can think about adding the first fish. Bear in mind that you are introducing them into an environment where very little biological activity is taking place. The natural cycles that will sustain the fish only start to mature once the fish have been added, although you can accelerate the process by adding a filter start product as explained on page 96.

Nevertheless, there is always a chance that the first fish will be exposed to less-than-perfect water conditions during the maturation process, so it is important to select species that are known to be hardy. This means that they are able to tolerate changes in water quality during the maturation process. It is not an excuse for allowing the water quality to deteriorate, as any fish will suffer in poor conditions. Indeed, if anything, you should tend the system with extra care in the early days to ensure that the water quality remains as good as possible for the first fish.

### The first fish

While the choice of first fish is open to debate and everyone has their own favorites, the fish featured on pages 112–115 are good candidates for consideration. Always bear in mind that even though their hardiness is one of the principal reasons for choosing them, first fish will form part of the finished display and you need to consider how they will coexist with the species you decide to add later on. As happens in nature, not all living creatures will live happily together. Always ask if the fish you want to buy are suitable for a community aquarium. This avoids the risk of buying a beautiful fish that eats all the other occupants of the tank within 24 hours!

### Buying fish

You can buy the equipment for your aquarium from anywhere, but when it comes to buying the fish, you must be satisfied that they are coming from an

**Left:** *Taping the corners of the bag ensures that there is no risk of small fish becoming trapped. The top of the bag should be securely knotted. Hold it firmly while transporting the fish.*

### How many fish should I buy the first time?

Because the aquarium is only in its settling down period, adding a large number of fish could overwhelm the system, causing water quality problems and fish deaths. The number of fish you can add depends on the size of your aquarium and the method of maturation (see page 98–101 for detailed information on this), but it is best to stick to a small number — usually between four and ten fish. Leave at least a week before introducing the next fish.

**Below:** *Shoaling fish, such as these zebra danios, settle down into a new aquarium more quickly if introduced as a group.*

**Below:** *Following a short journey home, float the unopened bags in the aquarium for about 20 minutes to allow the water temperatures to equalize before releasing the fish.*

**Above:** *If the journey home was long, first roll down the sides of the bag into a collar to allow stale air to escape. Some fishkeepers turn off the aquarium lights at this stage to avoid stressing the fish.*

*Although this is a potentially stressful time for fish, they should recover quite quickly.*

**Below:** *Float the bags in the aquarium for about 20 minutes. Check whether the water temperatures have equalized by dipping your finger first into the bag and then the tank.*

outlet that sells good-quality, really healthy stock. It is worth visiting all your local retailers to compare the quality and price of fish. As a guide, consider the following points when choosing a retailer:

- The retailer should have a licence to sell live animals.
- The retailer should be a member of an aquatic trade association with rules on keeping its livestock. This is evidence of a professional business that takes its responsibilities seriously.
- Is the shop clean? Are all the aquariums clean, inside and out? This shows a high degree of care by the shop.
- Even the best stores might experience fish losses, but several dead or diseased fish on display is not a good sign. Do not buy any apparently healthy fish from

an aquarium with diseased fish in it. The chances are that all the fish will be affected. Ideally, fish in quarantine should not be on display.

- All the tanks should have labels detailing the fish species they contain, their price, potential size, any special food requirements, compatibility with other fish and any special requirement, such as "likes plenty of plant cover."
- Look at the fish; do they look bright, healthy and interested in their surroundings? Are they behaving normally?
- Are the fish guaranteed? Most shops will offer some kind of guarantee, but

once the fish leave the shop you are entirely responsible for them and their environment. Any guarantee may involve testing the water in your aquarium should there be a problem.

- If possible, watch another customer buying fish and observe the staff. They should handle the fish as little as possible to minimize stress.

## Taking your fish home

Your retailer will transfer your chosen fish to one or more plastic bags, with enough water to cover them, and then fill the rest of the bag with air before sealing it. If the journey home is less than an hour, the fish

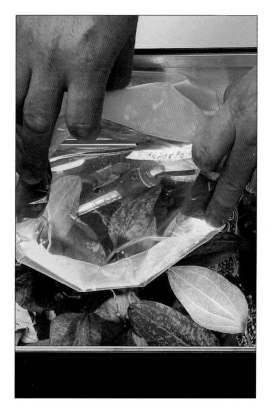

**Above:** *Hold the bag just below the water surface, tipping it slightly to encourage the fish to swim out in their own time. Make sure they are all released. Repeat the process with each bag of fish.*

will be fine with just air in the bag. If it is any longer, the retailer should fill the bag with oxygen. Finally, the retailer should tape the corners of the bag to ensure that no fish become trapped. For safe transportation, it is a good idea to take a cardboard box with you to the shop to contain the bags on the journey home.

Once you have found a good retailer you can choose your first fish with confidence. They will bring life and movement to the backdrop provided by the plants and become the real stars of the living picture you have created. All the first fish are top to midwater swimmers so will add instant interest.

**Above:** *These two pentazona barbs are soon swimming around the aquarium, investigating their new surroundings. Some fish are more timid and may hide away at first, but this is quite natural.*

**Left:** *With all the starter fish installed, the tank is now home to five zebra danios, five harlequin rasboras and three pentazona barbs. Do not be surprised if they do not show their best colors straightaway. These will improve as the fish become more confident in their new surroundings.*

## Stocking levels

As a rule of thumb, work on the basis of 1 cm (0.4 in) of fish (excluding the tail) for every one liter of water. This means that to an aquarium with a water volume of 150 liters you can add a maximum of 150 cm (60 in) of fish. This may seem quite high, but the calculation is based on the maximum adult size of the fish. This is why it is important to be aware of how big your fish will grow, and to build up the stock gradually. For example, zebra danios can reach a maximum size of 5 cm (2 in). If you add six individuals to the tank, you will have accounted for 30 cm of ultimate fish length, even though each young fish only measures 2 cm (0.8 in) when it first goes into the aquarium.

As a guide, never add more than 40 cm (16 in) of adult-sized fish at any one time. This will allow the biological filter to mature so that it can process their waste. Monitor the water quality until both the ammonia and nitrite levels have again reduced to zero before adding more fish. This is the only way to be sure that your filter has matured sufficiently to process the waste produced by all the fish in the aquarium.

# FIRST FISH

The first fish you add to the aquarium immediately bring color, movement and drama to the display. They are all midwater or upper-layer swimmers and will add interest to an area of the display perhaps not yet reached by the growing plants. The species described here include danios, rasboras, tetras and barbs and are hardier than most, but still require care and attention. It does not mean that all the fish in these groups are suitable for consideration as first fish. For example, certain tetras should be added only when the tank has been running for several weeks, if not longer. Other representatives of these groups of fish will be examined in more detail later in the book, as second or third fish. Just as you planned the decor and planting of your aquarium, it is worth thinking ahead about the fish you may wish to add in the future. Looking at the second and third fish options, and deciding which ones you like, may help you decide which species to start with, as they will all need to fit in together in the final display. For this reason, it also pays to discuss your future choices with your retailer when you buy the first fish. At this time, remember to include food and a net if you do not have these items already. Finally, follow the buying guidelines on page 108 and do not rush into buying fish you suspect are not healthy.

### ◀ Leopard Danio
*Brachydanio rerio* var. *frankei*

This variety of the zebra danio has spots along its flanks instead of stripes. It will mix happily with zebra danios and has the same temperament as its close cousin. In common with all danios, it has a pair of barbels on each side of its mouth that it uses to find food. This is simply a question of do you prefer spots or stripes? Maximum adult size: 6 cm (2.4 in).

### Zebra Danio ▲
*Brachydanio rerio*

As its name implies, this danio has distinctive horizontal stripes along each flank. Zebra danios are very lively schooling fish that swim at all levels and prefer a well-planted aquarium in which they can dart from cover to cover. They will thrive best in a school of six or more and are a popular choice for community aquariums. Originating from eastern India, they prefer neutral to slightly acid water conditions, although captive-bred specimens will tolerate a much wider pH range. Zebra danios are also available in a long-finned variety. Maximum adult size: 6 cm (2.4 in).

## ◀ **Black Widow Tetra**
*Gymnocorymbus ternetzi*

The black widow tetra is an excellent starter fish. Originating from South America, this peaceful schooling fish appreciates the cover of bushy plants and the shade generated by tall species. Younger fish can be identified by their striking black coloration, while older specimens appear gray. The black widow tetra tolerates one of the widest ranges of pH of any aquarium fish, so should suit almost any setup. Keep in groups of six. Maximum adult size: 5 cm (2 in).

## **Harlequin Rasbora** ▶
*Rasbora heteromorpha*

The harlequin is a small lively fish from Southeast Asia that is ideal for all sizes of community aquarium. It has a distinctive black triangle on the rear of the body and shows its best colors when kept in a group of at least six. The fish prefer to swim in the upper half of the aquarium and enjoy the cover provided by floating plants. For a small fish, the harlequin has a huge appetite and will readily feed on flake food. Maximum adult size: 4 cm (1.6 in).

## ◀ **Pearl Danio**
*Brachydanio albolineatus*

This is another peaceful species of danio and is ideal for a community aquarium. It is similar in shape to the zebra and leopard danio, with a pearly iridescence shot through with blue and purple. The females are larger and more colorful than males. Pearl danios originate from Southeast Asia and a pH of 6–7.5 would reflect their natural water conditions, but captive-bred specimens will tolerate a much wider range. They are best kept in a shoal but make sure your tank has a tight-fitting cover, as pearl danios like to jump. Color varieties are available. Maximum adult size: females 6 cm (2.4 in); males slightly smaller.

## **Galaxy Rasbora** ▲
*Danio margaritatus*

The galaxy rasbora was discovered in 2006 and very quickly became a popular aquarium fish. It has many great features: a peaceful shoaling nature, beautiful colors, and is easy to keep and stays very small. In common with many danios, they prefer to be in small groups of around six. Males have brighter blue flanks than females and will develop intense red bellies when they are spawning. They will thrive in a planted tank, though because of their diminutive size do not keep them with larger fish that might regard them as a snack. Maximum adult size: 2 cm (0.8 in).

### Pentazona Barb ❯

*Barbus pentazona pentazona*

The pentazona barb sports vivid stripes similar to those of the less sociable tiger barb. It constantly roams the aquarium looking for food and always seems interested in its surroundings. Beyond requiring good water quality during the maturation process, this very undemanding species is ideal for the beginner. It will thrive best in a group of five or six and is an excellent choice for all but the smallest community aquariums. Maximum adult size: 5 cm (2 in).

### Cherry Barb ▼

*Barbus titteya*

The cherry barb is one of the smallest barbs, but makes up for its lack of size with a stunning red body that serves it well in its natural habitat of shady Sri Lankan streams. These fish enjoy the cover provided by dense planting and the shade of floating plants. Introduce a group of five or six because cherry barbs can be timid if kept on their own. These peaceful fish are suitable for any community aquarium. Make sure their diet includes some flake food containing spirulina algae to keep the body color bright. Maximum adult size: 5 cm (2 in).

*The male's red coloration deepens during the breeding season.*

*Females are more orange in color and have a deeper belly.*

## ❤ Lemon, or Yellow, Tetra

*Hyphessobrycon pulchripinnis*

This is one of the more robust tetras. It is easy to keep in a community aquarium — ideally in groups of six or more — and will tolerate a wide range of pH values. Like most tetras, it enjoys the cover of heavy planting that mimics its natural habitat of woodland streams in Brazil. A color-enhancing food containing spirulina algae will help maintain its yellow coloration. Maximum adult size: 4.5 cm (1.8 in).

## ❮ Golden Barb

*Barbus semifasciolatus*

This lively, butter-colored barb from southeastern China will feel at home amongst dense vegetation. Grouping together several *Cryptocoryne* plants will achieve this effect in the aquarium. Keep this peaceful barb in a group of five or six individuals in any community aquarium. Maximum adult size: 10 cm (4 in).

## Silver-tipped Tetra ❯

*Hasemania nana*

These very striking tetras from the small streams of the Sao Francisco and Purus rivers in Brazil have the perfect streamlined body for life in fast-flowing waters. For this reason, they will enjoy the outlet flow from your power filter. Despite their small size, they are often one of the stars of the display. As well as plenty of swimming space, they will also appreciate the cover of plants to feel secure. These schooling fish are best kept in groups of at least six. Maximum adult size: 5 cm (2 in).

*Silver-tipped tetra (male)*

*Silver-tipped tetra (female)*

**During the following two weeks the aquarium will be settling down, ready to receive the second selection of fish.** ▶

# INCREASING THE FISH POPULATION

Once the aquarium has settled down and has been running with the first fish in it for a couple of weeks, you can think about adding more fish. As before, it is essential that you introduce any new fish a few at a time. This gives the bacteria in the filtration system a chance to increase gradually, so that they are able to break down the waste produced by the new fish. In addition to your usual testing regime, you must test for ammonia and nitrite levels regularly during the week following any fish introductions. This will allow you to take any remedial action necessary should the water quality deteriorate to an unacceptable level during this maturation process.

Another point to consider is the health of the new fish you are buying and whether you need to quarantine them at home in a separate tank. This was not necessary with the first fish, as they were "quarantined" in the display aquarium. Even if they had been carrying any disease organisms, there were no fish there to pass them on to. The second — and any subsequent fish additions — are different, as they may bring diseases into the display tank and not only succumb themselves, but also pass on the problem to the existing healthy fish.

Five weeks of growth on the plants in your display will have started to show, however you should check the plants for any dead leaves or others that have started to yellow, as these should be removed to prevent them rotting in the aquarium. The plants will respond to the continued injection of carbon dioxide and the introduction of liquid feeds to continue to flourish and grow toward their full potential.

**Right:** *When transferring new fish from a quarantine tank to the main display aquarium, you may need to use a plastic bag rather than a net if the two systems are in different rooms. Use a clean bag and tape the corners as before.*

*The existing fish are curious about their new companions, as these swim away from the plastic bag used to bring them from quarantine.*

# QUARANTINE

Even though you should be buying your fish from a reputable dealer who keeps them in the best possible conditions, it is a good strategy to quarantine any second and subsequent fish that you introduce.

## The quarantine tank

Depending on the size of the fish you intend buying, a quarantine tank should measure at least 45x25x25 cm (18x10x10 in). Do not quarantine more than six 5 cm (2 in) fish at any one time in a tank this size, as you will not be able to control the water quality and maintain the excellent conditions required in the quarantine tank. If any individual fish is more than 10 cm (4 in) long, you will need a larger tank.

Like the display aquarium, the quarantine tank must be equipped with heating, filtration and lighting equipment, plus some aeration. An air-powered filter is ideal in a small aquarium, as it filters, aerates and circulates the water. It is also worthwhile including some decor to provide cover for

the fish; very few species are happy in a bare aquarium.

## Caring for the fish

When you bring the new fish home from the shop, add them to the quarantine tank, following the same procedure as described on pages 108–109 for adding the first fish to the display aquarium. From now on you must care for them exactly as if they were in the main aquarium, with daily feeding, weekly water changes and other regular maintenance to ensure that they remain in the best possible conditions.

Strictly speaking, you should keep a fish in isolation for longer than the longest incubation period of any disease organism that could affect it. In real terms this could amount to a considerable period, as some viral diseases can lie dormant for a long time. For practical purposes, therefore, quarantine is dictated by the development period of the common pathogens most likely to affect aquarium fish. Generally,

20 days is adequate to quarantine new stock fish. During this time they can recover from their stressful capture and journey home, and can be treated for any common pathogens if they show symptoms (see pages 192–193).

## Monitoring the water quality

While the fish are in quarantine, check the water quality regularly. The pH level should match that of the main aquarium, unless a new fish has come from a retailer whose water is not the same as yours. In this case, alter the pH level until it is the same as in your display aquarium over the 20-day period. Do not subject fish to a daily change in pH of more than 0.3 of a unit. Maintain ammonia and nitrite levels at zero, with nitrate below 25 mg/l.

If there are no signs of disease after 20 days, you can transfer the fish to the main display aquarium. Always monitor the water quality in the main aquarium once the new fish have been added. To help the filter cope with the extra waste, add your

## A quarantine tank

*Include a clean clay flowerpot or artificial decor item that will provide a refuge for nervous or poorly fish.*

*Use a heater-thermostat to maintain the water temperature at the same level as the main display aquarium.*

*This simple internal filter is ideal for a quarantine tank. The twin sponges will sustain a useful population of beneficial bacteria to keep the water clean.*

*This air pump "powers" the internal sponge filter.*

*Some fish, such as Corydoras and many loaches, appreciate some substrate. However, it is difficult to keep substrates clean, and they can give refuge to some diseases that might appear while you are quarantining your fish. Mid- and surface- dwelling fish will be happy with a clean bottom to the tank. Judge whether to include a thin layer of substrate on a case-by-case basis depending on the fish.*

filter start-up product a couple of days before you add the new fish. Follow the dosage rate recommended.

## Keeping the tank ready

As the quarantine tank will not always be in use, there will be long periods when it is left empty, and the filter bacteria will die without a constant source of waste from fish. This may cause problems when you want to use the quarantine tank again, since an unmatured filter is likely to result in water quality problems that will harm new fish already stressed from transport. Adding fish food to the tank to keep bacteria alive is not recommended as it will result in the decomposition of leftover waste food, providing an ideal home for harmful fungal and bacterial diseases to thrive. You can keep the tank matured by adding regular doses of live bacteria, but this is wasteful and time-consuming as well as costly in terms of the electricity used to continue running the filter and heater. A better option is to switch off the quarantine tank and bring it back into use when it is needed. To do this without encountering the problems of an unmatured tank, you can fill the quarantine tank with mature water from the main tank. This has the added benefit that the quarantine tank will now have water of exactly the same chemistry as the main aquarium.

There are several ways of ensuring that the quarantine tank's filter is also matured when it is needed. You can run the quarantine tank filter inside the main tank as an additional filter when the quarantine tank is not in use, and simply move the filter over when it is needed. If you are using an external filter on your main tank, there may be space for one of the sponges from the quarantine tank's filter. Place this in the external filter, where it will house a population of bacteria and remove it for use in the quarantine tank when needed. A final option is to reseed the quarantine tank filter when it is needed using a live bacteria product. This, combined with the use of mature

tank water, should allow you to get the quarantine tank up and running at short notice when it is needed for new fish or to house sick fish from the main tank.

## Keep equipment separate

Keep a separate supply of equipment for the quarantine tank and never transfer any items used in the quarantine tank to the main display aquarium. You can quite easily pass a pathogen from sick fish to your main display aquarium on a wet net. If you do need to use any equipment in both aquariums be sure to disinfect it between each use.

## Other uses

There are several occasions when you will find a quarantine tank very useful. If a fish becomes sick or distressed, it will benefit from the isolation of the quarantine tank, which then becomes a hospital tank. You will be able to inspect the fish closely and treat it as required before returning it to the main aquarium.

Some fish can become territorial, usually when breeding. They may pick on one of the more docile members of the display if it ventures too close to their eggs or offspring. An injured fish quickly succumbs to secondary bacterial and fungal infections, so remove it to the sanctuary

### Fish swaps

Some retailers may be willing to take young fish off your hands and offer you a token credit for them in the form of aquarium equipment or food. Do not expect to get a retail price for them; after all, the retailer is doing you a favor and helping to find new homes for the fish. Always arrange a fish swap in advance to avoid moving (and therefore stressing) the fish unnecessarily if the retailer does not have space for them when you arrive at the shop.

of the quarantine aquarium until the aggressive tendencies of the breeding pair subside. A bullied or injured fish can thus regain its strength before being returned to the main display.

If any fry are produced in the main aquarium, they will quickly come under attack from all the other fish (including even their parents), which regard them as a source of live food. If you wish to save the fry and grow them, remove them to the quarantine aquarium. This can act as a nursery until they are large enough to be housed with other fish.

**Left:** *Among the second fish to be added to the aquarium are some corydoras catfish. Float the bag in the quarantine tank for 20 minutes to equalize the water temperatures before releasing them.*

**Right:** *Tilt the bag gently and allow the catfish to swim away. A period in the quarantine tank will enable you to check the fish for any latent disease or health problem before they go into the main aquarium.*

# BARBS

The colorful and active barbs have long been popular choices for the home aquarium, but you should choose them with care to ensure their compatibility with the other fish in the tank. Retailers stock many species, and there is a wide range of body shapes, colors and temperaments to choose from. The cherry barb, for example, adds a flush of color to the display and being one of the smaller barbs, is suitable for almost any aquarium. The tiger barb, on the other hand, while enjoying huge popularity because of its stunning colorful markings, will only be a suitable addition if you choose its tankmates with care. Nevertheless, in the right company it will become a focal point in the aquarium. Barbs readily shoal with members of their own species, and this behavior adds considerable interest to any display. Be sure to keep shoaling species in groups of six individuals or more so that they feel secure. These fish will readily take flake foods. When the larger fish reach maturity, offer them pellets. You can offer freeze-dried live foods, such as bloodworm and brineshrimp, as a treat.

## Arulius Barb ⌄

*Barbus arulius*

The arulius barb from India is a sociable species that prefers to be kept in a small group. For this reason, and also because it is one of the bigger barb species, it is best suited to the larger community tank. The arulius barb is placid, however, and can be kept with all but the smallest of tankmates. Males have a distinctive threadlike dorsal fin that adds a different texture to the display. As the fish matures, the body develops a purple-blue color along the back, with black bars that act as part of the fish's natural camouflage. If the fish is not happy in the aquarium, the purple blue fades to a dull gray. Maximum adult size: 12 cm (4.7 in).

## Silver Shark ⌃

*Balantiocheilus melanopterus*

This stunning-looking fish from Thailand and Borneo gets its common name from its sharklike body shape. However, its temperament is peaceful and the silver shark can be kept with the smallest of fish. The distinctive silver body with black-edged fins makes a marked contrast to more colorful tankmates. This member of the carp family grows quite large, so is really only suited to tanks over 120 cm (48 in) long. Do not be fooled by small specimens offered for sale; they will grow and need a large tank with plenty of swimming space to be happy. Silver sharks are active and can be prone to jumping; be sure to provide a tight-fitting hood on the aquarium. Offer pellets to larger fish. Maximum adult size: 35 cm (14 in).

## Rosy Barb ▼
*Barbus conchonius*

The chief attraction of these undemanding fish from India is their coloring: males are gold with bright red flanks, while the females are all gold. Since they do not need the reassurance of living in a shoal, but are quite happy in pairs, they are ideal for the smaller display. Like most barbs, they enjoy a certain degree of plant cover as well as room to swim. These "gilt-edged" fish are a valuable addition to any community aquarium. Maximum adult size: 7 cm (2.75 in).

## Tiger Barb ▲
*Barbus tetrazona*

With their bold stripes and red tips to the fins and nose, tiger barbs make a stunning addition to a community tank. They are also available in green and albino forms. However, these very active fish from Indonesia, Sumatra and Borneo require some care if they are not to ruin your display. They are shoaling fish with a defined hierarchy within the shoal. Always keep them in a group of at least six individuals because lone specimens can cause a nuisance in the aquarium by nipping at the fins of other fish. Do not house them with fish that have long flowing fins, such as Siamese fighting fish and gouramis, or with slow swimmers, such as Angelfish. If you are prepared to cater for their needs, tiger barbs make a lively contribution to the aquarium. Maximum adult size: 7 cm (2.75 in).

## Cuming's Barb ▶
*Barbus cumingi*

These very lively fish enjoy plenty of swimming space and will take advantage of an open area in the planting scheme. Cuming's barbs have a reticulated pattern on each scale that makes them stand out from similar fish. Other attractive features are the bright red dorsal and anal fins and the two false eyespots on each side of the flanks that serve as a deterrent to predators in their natural Sri Lankan habitat. They do best when kept in a small shoal, and since they remain relatively small, they can be included in any size of display without creating problems. This is a peaceful barb that will not bother with fish outside its own species. Maximum adult size: 5 cm (2 in).

## Black Ruby Barb ❯

*Barbus nigrofasciatus*

If tiger barbs appeal to you but you do not feel you can supply their needs, then black ruby barbs from Sri Lanka would make a wonderful alternative addition to your community aquarium. They have a similar body shape, with black vertical bars along the body. However, instead of red fins they have a rosy red glow that begins at the nose and spreads along each flank. The black fins are a contrast to the rouge body. The black ruby barb enjoys the cover provided by plant growth and can be timid if unable to find shade away from bright lighting. It prefers to be kept in a small shoal. Maximum adult size: 6.5 cm (2.5 in).

## Clown Barb ▼

*Barbus everetti*

The body shape of this attractive barb is slightly different to that of other community barbs in that it is more elongated. The fish is gold, with dark spots or bands along the flanks, while the red fins further increase the clown barb's appeal. Although it prefers the slightly acid water conditions found in its native habitat in Singapore and Borneo, your retailer may have specimens adapted to the local water conditions. Although non-aggressive, this lively barb will roam the aquarium, adding variety and interest. Prefers to be kept in a small shoal, but can be kept in pairs. Maximum adult size: 10 cm (4 in).

## Checkered Barb ▶

*Barbus oligolepis*

This wonderful little barb has a striking reticulated pattern on each scale that gives the flanks a checkerboard appearance. The males are a little bolder in color, with reddish brown fins outlined in black. The fish look their best in a small shoal, patrolling the aquarium but never venturing too far from plant cover. The checkered barb from Indonesia and Sumatra is not only handsome, but also one of the most peaceful barbs, so well worth considering for any community display. Maximum adult size: up to 15 cm (6 in), but more commonly 5–7 cm (2–2.75 in).

## ◀ Odessa Barb

*Barbus ticto*

Male Odessa barbs develop into stunning fish, with a bright red band along each side and a false black eyespot on each flank. Each scale has a reticulated pattern, so the flanks of the fish stand out well in the aquarium. Juvenile specimens offered for sale seldom display any adult coloration, so you must buy them in good faith, in the expectation that they will mature into handsome aquarium specimens. Although they will live happily in pairs, a small group of these peaceful barbs, which originate from India and Sri Lanka, will always make more of an impact in a community display. Maximum adult size: 10 cm (4 in).

## Blue-Barred Barb ▲
*Barbus barilioides*

Although this very lively fish from Angola and Zimbabwe enjoys swimming freely, it will spend a lot of time under cover if the aquarium lighting is too bright. Given its placid nature, it should be kept in a small shoal of eight or more, otherwise individuals become shy and will not thrive. The vivid dark blue stripes are a distinctive feature. This fish is ideally suited to smaller community aquariums, but it will need generous swimming space. Maximum adult size: 5 cm (2 in).

## Black-Spot Barb ▼
*Barbus filamentosus*

The black-spot is a beautiful small barb, very active throughout the aquarium and worth considering as an alternative to the tiger barb if you are worried about the latter's potentially disruptive behavior. Juveniles have distinct two-bar markings on a gold background, as well as bright red flashes on the dorsal fin and tail lobes. As they grow, the fish lose the black bar through the middle of the body, but retain the black spot near the tail. Always look for examples with two black bars; being the younger fish, you can then enjoy watching their colors change as they mature. These peaceful barbs from India and Sri Lanka need a large tank and prefer slightly acid water, but your aquarium shop should have specimens acclimatized to your local water conditions. It creates a better display in a group of six or more. Offer floating foods. Maximum adult size: 15 cm (6 in).

# RASBORAS

Rasboras, a hardy group of fish from Asia, are part of the carp family. Their peaceful but active behavior, along with colorful markings, make them ideal for the community aquarium. The most common member of the family, the harlequin rasbora, is an excellent starter fish (see page 113). Other members of the family are less commonly seen in aquarium shops but just as suited to a display. They include the clown rasbora (*Rasbora kalochroma*) and the dwarf rasbora (*Rasbora maculata*). Rasboras are easy to feed on flake food; they also enjoy a treat of freeze-dried live foods, such as bloodworm and brineshrimp.

## Scissortail Rasbora ❯

*Rasbora trilineata*

A unique tail pattern, combined with its swimming action, make this active fish look like a small pair of scissors swimming through the aquarium. The impression is reinforced when repeated throughout a small shoal and will make a strong impact in your display. The silver, black and white coloration of the scissortail contrasts well with the brighter colors of many other community fish. These rasboras from Malaysia, Sumatra and Borneo will enjoy open swimming spaces in your planting scheme. Do not mix them with boisterous barbs. Maximum adult size: up to 15 cm (6 in), but rarely more than 7–8 cm (2.75–3.2 in).

### ❮ Clown Rasbora

*Rasbora kalochroma*

This sleek little fish, with its distinctive black spot marking, adds finesse to the display. However, despite their undoubted presence, the lovely clown rasboras can become a little possessive of a particular area within the aquarium. The solution is to keep them in a group of six or more with plenty of other fish, so that they do not get a chance to set up a territory. Their natural home is in Malaysia, Sumatra and Borneo and they prefer well-planted surroundings in which they can shelter from bright lighting. Maximum adult size: up to 10 cm (4 in), but rarely more than 7–8 cm (2.75–3.2 in).

### ▲ Red-Striped Rasbora

*Rasbora pauciperforata*

These bright, lively individuals are best kept with fish of a similar disposition, as they feel more secure in numbers. However, you should also provide good planting so that they can reach cover should they feel the need. The bright red stripe along each flank adds to the pattern mix that other fish in the aquarium might not provide, so this rasbora is worth adding to any community display — ideally in a group of eight or more. Originating from Southeast Asia, Malaysia and Sumatra, it prefers slightly acid water, but your local retailer may have some examples that have been acclimatized to your local water conditions. Offer softened algae wafers in addition to the usual aquarium foods. Maximum adult size: 7 cm (2.75 in).

# DANIOS

Danios are among the hardiest aquarium fish and an excellent choice for newcomers to the hobby. They are ideal starter fish, easy to feed and look after. Danios are always busying themselves around the tank in search of food and this lively behavior makes them very endearing subjects for community aquariums. They will not eat any of the aquarium plants and will not grow large enough to disrupt any aquarium decor. There are several species to choose from, but the zebra and the leopard danio (page 112) are the most frequently sold. Long-finned varieties of both have been bred, but are not as appealing as the natural forms of the danio or other species of fish with naturally long fins. Danios are best kept in a small shoal to help them feel secure.

## Giant Danio ▼
*Danio aequipinnatus*

As its name suggests, this is a larger species of danio and much deeper-bodied than its slender cousins, the Zebra and Leopard Danio. It sports lovely trout-style markings down each flank on a background of turquoise-blue that stands out in the aquarium. The Giant Danio, from Malaysia, Sumatra and Borneo, has an upturned mouth, an indication that it often feeds from the surface in the wild. In the aquarium, it will readily adapt to manufactured floating foods. This lively, active species is happiest living in a small shoal in an aquarium at least 1 m (39 in) long. Make sure it is securely covered, as these active fish are liable to jump out.

Maximum adult size: 10 cm (4 in).

# TETRAS

Most of the following species are naturally shoaling. so to create the best effect, include a dozen or more individuals in a single display. Do not add them all at once, however, as the water quality will suffer. To avoid major problems, introduce them in small groups of three or four individuals, thus allowing the filter to adjust gradually to the extra load of new fish.

## Emperor Tetra ▼
*Nematobrycon palmeri*

For something really different, consider adding the stunning emperor tetra from Colombia to your aquarium. It is one of the few fish that will add a touch of purple to the display, a color that stands out against the greens and reds of the plants. Its aggressive-looking expression hides a placid nature, so do not keep it with any large, boisterous fish. For a tetra, the emperor is a long-lived fish, surviving up to six years in a well-cared-for display.

Maximum adult size: 5 cm (2 in).

*The giant danio is a fast-swimming surface dweller.*

*Gold giant danio, a color form bred for the aquarium hobby.*

## ▼ Cardinal Tetra
*Paracheirodon axelrodi*

In the cardinal tetra, the red band runs the entire length of the fish, making it slightly more colorful than the neon, if that is possible. For a special display in a suitable aquarium, keep these fish in a large shoal of 25 to 30 or more. Many displays look best with little in the way of other midwater swimmers, giving the cardinals exclusive rights to this area of the aquarium. This way the fish will exhibit the natural shoaling behavior seen in their native Brazilian habitat. However, they can be included in a mixed aquarium (but not with larger potentially aggressive fish), where a minimum of six individuals will add to the overall display, yet still feel secure. Maximum adult size: 5 cm (2 in).

## ▼ Neon Tetra
*Paracheirodon innesi*

This stunning little tetra from Peru brings visual delight to a display and is probably the most popular aquarium fish ever kept. The almost unnaturally vibrant red and neon-blue flashes are seen to best effect when a group of at least six individuals demonstrate their natural shoaling behavior, and a brilliant display can be achieved with a dozen or more. Do not house them with larger fish that may pick off the neon tetra as a dietary supplement. Angelfish, for example, have a habit of doing this, so do not keep them in the same aquarium. Maximum adult size: 4 cm (1.6 in).

## Bleeding ▲ Heart Tetra
*Hyphessobrycon erythrostigma*

The red spot just below the lateral line gives the bleeding heart tetra its common name, and the unusual diamond-shaped body adds another dimension to the aquarium display. These large tetras from Peru can be kept in a pair instead of a group, but in a large tank they certainly make an impact in a shoal. Males can be identified by extended dorsal and anal fins. The fish prefer water with a pH level between 6.5 and 7.2. However your aquarium shop may have specimens acclimatized to your local water conditions. Bleeding heart tetras prefer a quiet aquarium, so avoid including them with busier, larger fish and potentially aggressive species. Maximum adult size: 6 cm (2.4 in).

### Glowlight Tetra ❯

*Hemigrammus erythrozonus*

The glowlight tetra from Guyana adds a brilliant flash of orange-pink to the aquarium display. The unusual coloration (for a tetra) makes this placid fish stand out from the crowd and explains why it is so popular. The color stripe runs the entire length of the body, including parts of the eye and tail. The colors look their brightest against the dense planting these fish prefer. Keep the glowlight in a shoal of at least six individuals. Maximum adult size: 4 cm (1.6 in).

### Head-and-Tail Light Tetra ▼

*Hemigrammus ocellifer*

The common name of this peaceful tetra from Guyana and Bolivia comes from the two shiny patches of skin close to the head and tail. As with most tetras, the head-and-tail light prefers to live in a shoal of six to eight individuals. In ideal conditions, these fish are likely to spawn in the community aquarium. Maximum adult size: 4.5 cm (1.8 in).

## Black Neon Tetra ▼

*Hyphessobrycon herbertaxelrodi*

Although distinctly different from the neon tetra, the black neon from Brazil is similar in body shape. It sports a pale green stripe alongside a predominantly black one and these unusual colors are complemented by red on the top half of the eye. The black neon is more demanding in terms of aquarium conditions than most of its cousins. Ideally, the pH should be on the low side for a community aquarium — between 6.5 and 7.5 — but your aquarium shop may stock specimens that are acclimatized to your local water conditions. Keep a minimum of six individuals. Maximum adult size: 4 cm (1.6 in).

## ▼ Serpae Tetra

*Hyphessobrycon callistus*

The serpae tetra is a bright-red, active fish that brings constant movement to the display. Being undemanding in terms of conditions, it may represent a better option than the red phantom tetra. However, being more boisterous, it should be kept in a shoal of at least six or more individuals to ensure that any bickering remains within the shoal and does not affect other fish in the display. This tetra from Paraguay makes a good, colorful addition to any aquarium. Maximum adult size: 4 cm (1.6 in).

129

## Flame Tetra ▼

*Hyphessobrycon flammeus*

The male flame tetra is particularly striking, with a bright red anal fin and lower body, while the rest of the body is a dusky red. The females are more subdued in coloration. This easy-care, peaceful fish is worth considering as an alternative to the red phantom tetra, which can be more delicate. Do not be deterred if these peaceful Brazilian fish do not show their full colors in the shop; once settled in a planted aquarium, they will color up. Keep a minimum of six individuals. Maximum adult size: 4 cm (1.6 in).

## Red-Eyed Tetra ▶

*Moenkhausia sanctaefilomenae*

The upper half of this fish's eye is bright red, hence the common name. But this bold-looking tetra also has a distinctive black band across the tail and dark-edged scales that give it an almost armor-plated appearance. These lovely shoaling fish from Brazil, Bolivia and Peru will swim toward the surface as well as in midwater and enjoy the cover provided in a well-planted aquarium. Being slightly bigger than most tetras, they are best suited to a larger aquarium if you plan to keep a shoal. Maximum adult size: 7 cm (2.75 in).

## ▼ Congo Tetra

*Phenacogrammus interruptus*

The Congo tetra from Zaire is a stylish addition to the aquarium. Its gold and grayish blue-green flanks are complemented, in the males only (shown here), by long flowing fins. It is one of the largest popular tetras, but despite its size, it is timid and should not be kept with boisterous fish. Congo tetras are best kept in a small shoal of six individuals in an aquarium measuring at least 90 cm (36 in), as they need plenty of swimming space. Provide an environment with relatively dense planting, although not fine-leaved plants, which they will nibble. Some surface plant cover will make the Congo tetras feel at home and encourage them to show off their colors. Maximum adult size: Males 8.5 cm (3.3 in), females slightly smaller.

## Buenos Aires Tetra ▼

*Hemigrammus caudovittatus*

This bold, colorful tetra from Argentina, Paraguay and Brazil is easy to keep and longlived by tetra standards, making it an excellent choice for the first-time aquarium keeper. All the fins, other than the dorsal, are bright red and the body is silver. A black bar runs from the base of the tail and between the lobes. The Buenos Aires tetra provides constant colorful movement in the aquarium. Its only potential drawback is a tendency to eat fine-leaved plants, so only keep it in a display with robust plants that can withstand some attention. Keep a minimum of six individuals. Maximum adult size: 7 cm (2.75 in).

# GOURAMIS

Gouramis are a peaceful group of fish that swim in the middle and upper layers of the aquarium. As most species have long, flowing fins, they should not be kept with other fish that have a tendency to fin nip. In the wild, gouramis live in swampy wetlands, where dissolved oxygen levels are low. In addition to using their gills, they also take in air at the surface and pass it into a convoluted labyrinth organ near the gill chamber that allows oxygen to pass into a network of tiny blood vessels. Gouramis share this ability with other "labyrinth fish" such as Siamese fighting fish.

## Kissing Gourami ▼

*Helostoma temminckii*

This fish's common name comes from its fleshy mouth and the behavior of "kissing" between two fish. The "kissing" is actually part of the fishes' fighting strategy, and the weaker fish normally gives in after a bout. Although fights are not uncommon, the fish are generally peaceful and can be kept singly or in groups. The mouth is also well designed to graze algae. Vegetable material is an important part of the diet and can be maintained with the addition of algae-based pellets and wafer foods. This fish will eat most aquarium plants. Kissing gouramis can reach 30 cm (12 in) in the wild and at least 20 cm (8 in) in captivity, requiring a 1.5–1.8 m (5–6 ft) tank, so they are not a fish to be chosen lightly.

## ❮ Pearl Gourami

*Trichogaster leeri*

The stunning coloration of the pearl gourami from Malaysia, Sumatra and Borneo helps to explain why it is one of the most popular gourami species. Each spotted flank has a jet black line running from the nose through the eye and all the way to the tail. As they mature, males (shown here) develop a red breast, the color stretching from the underside of the mouth to the start of the anal fin. Males also have extended, almost pointed dorsal fins, while those of females remain rounded. This will help you to select a pair, although most retailers only sell them as a pair. Pearl gouramis can be quite long-lived for aquarium species, surviving up to eight years, but they must be kept with other peaceful species if they are to fulfil their potential. They prefer to occupy the upper layers of the tank and enjoy the shelter of reasonably dense planting. Maximum adult size: 12 cm (4.7 in).

## Thick-Lipped Gourami ⋀

*Colisa labiosa*

The thick lips that give rise to this fish's common name are ideal for sucking in floating food and, indeed, it happily occupies the upper and middle parts of the aquarium. Its coloration is very similar to that of the dwarf gourami, with diagonal stripes of red and cobalt blue, but the thick lips are a clear distinguishing feature. Males (shown here) have the pointed dorsal fin seen in most gouramis, making the fish relatively easy to sex. Thick-lipped gouramis, native to India and Myanmar (Burma), are among the larger community species of gourami available. Provide slightly acid water conditions and keep with peaceful species only. Maximum adult size: 9 cm (3.5 in).

## ❮ Dwarf Gourami

*Colisa lalia*

The dwarf gourami, from India and Borneo, is one of the all-time classics for the small to medium-sized community aquarium. The color variants are immense, but the most popular are those with the natural diagonal red-and-cobalt blue stripes. Like other gouramis, they appreciate the protection of dense planting, especially the extra cover created by floating plants. They dislike being hassled by boisterous tankmates, so choose your stock carefully. Dwarf gouramis thrive better when kept in pairs. Females tend to have less vibrant colors than males (shown here), so ask your retailer to select a pair. Maximum adult size: 5 cm (2 in).

## Moonlight Gourami ❯

*Trichogaster microlepis*

This "ghost" of the aquarium is a pure silvery white, and like all gouramis, it has very elongated pelvic fins. In good specimens, these will carry the only other color seen on these fish: orange to red in males, yellow in the females. However, a much easier way to sex a pair is to identify the male by his extended, pointed dorsal fin. The moonlight gourami can become the target of fin-nipping fish, so keep it with peaceful species only and provide this timid fish from Thailand and Cambodia with the cover provided by dense planting. Maximum adult size: 15 cm (6 in).

## Snakeskin Gourami ▼

*Trichogaster pectoralis*

Small scales cover the body of *T. pectoralis*, hence its common name. The principal marking is the black stripe along the lateral line on each side of the fish. This is broken by some vertical silver stripes near the tail. In males, there is a red hue to the anal fin, while in females (shown here), it is yellow. The easiest way to identify a pair, however, is to look for the pointed dorsal fin of the male. The Snakeskin, from Malaysia, Thailand and Cambodia, grows relatively large, so is ideally suited to the larger, peaceful community aquarium. It is one of the most placid species. Maximum adult size: up to 20 cm (8 in).

### WARNING: One gourami to avoid

If you are ever tempted to buy a fish labelled as the common gourami (*Osphronemus gorami*), then please think again! *Osphronemus gorami* is a real giant of the fish world, growing to 70 cm (28 in) or more. Although it is a beautiful fish in its own right, it should only be kept in public aquariums and by fishkeepers who are dedicated to providing the necessary space and investment that these fish require. When small, *Osphronemus gorami* could be mistaken for a large chocolate gourami, so choose with care and ask your retailer for positive identification.

## Croaking Gourami ▼

*Trichopsis vittata*

The slender-bodied croaking gourami brings another dimension to the community aquarium, since both the male and female make croaking noises when displaying. They also add a rich tapestry of colors, including the familiar reds and cobalt blues. These timid fish from India, Thailand, Vietnam, Malaysia and Indonesia need surface planting for cover. Maximum adult size: 6.5 cm (2.5 in).

## Three-Spot Gourami ▼

*Trichogaster trichopterus*

The three-spot gourami makes a distinctive addition to an aquarium display. Two of the spots are black body markings against the blue skin, while the third is the eye. Together, these form its delicate camouflage. It is one of the most commonly available aquarium species and also one of the most sedentary, often only moving very slowly around the upper layers of the aquarium. As such, it is susceptible to the attentions of boisterous tankmates, so choose fellow species with care. The three-spot gourami, from Malaysia, Burma and Vietnam, will tolerate most water conditions. Selective breeding has produced a golden form that does not have spots and is sold as the golden gourami. Maximum adult size: 10 cm (4 in).

## ▲ Honey Gourami

*Colisa sota*

Being one of the smaller gourami species, the honey gourami from India, Assam and Bangladesh is ideally suited to the smaller setup. The glorious honey color is seen in the male, which also has a dark blue-black head and belly. To thrive, the honey gourami, prefers dense plant cover in which to hide. Like all gouramis, these fish can become territorial when they breed, so the plant cover helps to protect both them and other fish in the aquarium. Keep with peaceful species only. Maximum adult size: 5 cm (2 in).

135

# CATFISH

Catfish are a fascinating group of predominantly bottom-feeding fish that add movement to the lower area of the aquarium, and their varied patterns of behavior are a source of endless interest to the fishkeeper. For example, the busy *Corydoras* catfish spend a great deal of their time picking over the substrate looking for food, while the suckermouth species often sit and watch the proceedings in the tank before shuffling around to another vantage point. For balance and interest, suitable catfish should be included in every display.

## Corydoras

Even though nearly 200 Corydoras species are known to science, only a few dozen are available to aquarium hobbyists. The small size and placid nature of these South American catfish make them ideal community subjects, and their busy nature and often striking markings add further to their appeal. They are all peaceful species that can be mixed and matched as you wish, but in common with most fish, they create the most natural display and impact when seen as a shoal of the same species. Indeed, Corydoras never seem to thrive as individuals, so it is always a good idea to buy a small group.

If you intend keeping Corydoras catfish in your display, be sure to choose a smooth substrate material, as any sharp edges will wear away the barbels that they use to help them find food. Although they will scavenge food that has sunk out of reach of the other aquarium inhabitants, it is best to feed them directly to ensure they get enough. Offer them sinking tablet and wafer foods, with treats of freeze-dried livefoods, such as bloodworm and tubifex.

### *Corydoras duplicareus* ▲

This small *Corydoras* catfish from the Amazon River system can be difficult to find in aquarium shops but is worth pursuing. The body is a light sandy color with a jet black stripe down the back and another across the head to hide the eye. In between the two there is a stunning gold spot that contrasts well with the black markings. This *Corydoras* will take most foods, but include treats of freeze-dried or frozen bloodworm. Ensure your display has a section of open substrate on which these fish can forage. This peaceful species is a great addition to any community display. Maximum adult size: 5 cm (2 in).

### Bronze Corydoras ▼

*Corydoras aeneus*

Sporting deep bronze, armored scales, the bronze corydoras is a common sight in aquarium shops and an excellent choice for the beginner. Its industrious behavior is typical of this group; it enjoys scouring open areas of substrate for food and will keep foreground plants free of debris. This firm favorite with aquarium keepers worldwide is also available in an albino form, which makes a fine alternative to the bronze coloration. Maximum adult size: 7 cm (2.75 in).

### Artificially colored fish

Do not accept any albino fish that have been artificially colored, as this drastically reduces their life expectancy. By rejecting these fish, the unethical process of fish coloring can be discouraged.

## Harald Schultz's ▶ Corydoras
*Corydoras haraldschultzi*

This species closely resembles *C. sterbai*, although the colors are usually much darker. To tell them apart with certainty, look closely at the spots. *C. haraldschultzi* has dark spots on a light background, while *C. sterbai* has light spots on a dark background. In common with *C. sterbai*, it has yellow-gold front rays on the pectoral and pelvic fins, which can darken to orange in mature adults of both species. Maximum adult size: 7 cm (2.75 in).

## ▼ *Corydoras gossei*

This beautiful little catfish has a mottled head pattern, while the tail has an arrangement of broken stripes. The dark flanks contrast with the very pale underside and the whole body is highlighted by bright yellow leading edges to the dorsal and pectoral fins. *C. gossei* prefers slightly acid water, but your local shop may have some examples that are acclimatized to your local water conditions. In the aquarium, it looks even better when kept together with a group of *C. sterbai*. Maximum adult size: 6 cm (2.4 in).

## ▼ Peppered Corydoras
*Corydoras paleatus*

Along with the bronze corydoras, the peppered corydoras is another highly popular catfish and commonly available in the aquarium trade. The mottled patterns along each flank act as perfect camouflage in the wild. The white underside of the peppered corydoras is often visible as the fish scurry around the aquarium. An albino form is also available. Maximum adult size: 7 cm (2.75 in).

## Corydoras reticulatus ▼

The marbled pattern of this Peruvian corydoras works as effective camouflage in the wild, and adds an impressive element to the aquarium display. The dark flanks have silver markings, the dorsal fin is black with a silver stripe and the tail is also striped. *C. reticulatus* is one of the most attractive *Corydoras* species and suited to all but the smallest of displays. Keep some of the foreground substrate free of plants to allow the fish to forage and you can enjoy observing a small group bustling round the aquarium. Maximum adult size: 7 cm (2.75 in).

## Dwarf Corydoras ❯

*Corydoras pygmaeus*

Most *Corydoras* species inhabit the lower reaches of the aquarium, but unusually, *C. pygmaeus* spends most of its time swimming in the mid to upper layers. The fish are best kept in a group of half a dozen and are easy to identify by the black stripe that runs from nose to tail. In most *Corydoras* species the mouth is underslung, but in *C. pygmaeus* it is more forward facing. When it comes to feeding this baby of the *Corydoras* group, it is a good idea to crush up some flake food, so that it can feed easily in midwater. Watch the fish carefully to ensure that they receive enough food amongst the other busy midwater swimmers. Maximum adult size: 2.5 cm (1 in).

## Panda Corydoras

*Corydoras panda*

The panda is one of the smaller species of *Corydoras*, but easy to recognize by the black bands on the head, dorsal fin and caudal peduncle. These markings, set against a pale background, produce a striking and well-named addition to the display. *C. panda*, from Peru, has been known to spawn in the aquarium, but picking males and females may be difficult in the aquarium shop. Mature females are usually larger than males, but this difference will not be apparent in young fish. The best option is to buy a small group in the hope of acquiring at least one of each sex. Maximum adult size: 4.5 cm (1.8 in).

## Sterba's Corydoras

*Corydoras sterbai*

One of the stars of the *Corydoras* family, *C. sterbai* has a beautiful mottled pattern with white spots on its head and broken stripes along each flank that extend into the tail. This striking pattern is enhanced by the stunning golden leading edges to the pectoral and pelvic fins. To help the fish feel at home, make sure they have an area of open substrate to swim around. Maximum adult size: 8 cm (3.2 in).

# LOACHES

Although these fish belong to the same family as barbs and danios, they have evolved to live on the floor of their chosen habitat. The loaches forage in the aquarium substrate, feeding on particles of food missed by other fish. They still need feeding and will enjoy tablet and wafer foods, plus treats of freeze-dried or frozen bloodworms. They have underslung mouths surrounded by sensitive barbels that enable them to find their food by touch and taste. Loaches are generally peaceful, but some species should be avoided, as they will hassle other tankmates. The following species are ideal for a community display.

## Dwarf or Chain Loach

*Yasuhikotakia sidthimunki*

The dwarf loach, from India and Thailand, has a very pretty chain pattern along each flank that runs all the way from the characteristic underslung mouth to the tail. It is an ideal bottom-dwelling community fish, constantly active over the substrate looking for food and, like the clown loach, will perform a valuable service in picking off unwanted juvenile snails. Keeping these fish in a small group of four or five helps them to feel secure. For the same reason, you should make sure they have some hiding places. The dwarf loach's mature size makes it an excellent alternative to the clown loach if you are worried about the latter's potential size. Maximum adult size: 5.5 cm (2.2 in).

## Zebra Loach

*Botia striata*

This dramatic-looking fish is generally very peaceful. The more hiding places and cover you provide the better, because then it will feel secure and will be out and about most of the time. Ideally, keep zebra loaches as the only bottom dweller, as in some aquariums they become rather possessive of their own space! Like all loaches, they should be kept in groups of at least five or six. Maximum size 9 cm (3.5 in). *Yunnanilus cruciatus*, another striped loach, is very similar in all respects although about half the size of *B. striata*. It is particularly suitable for smaller tanks, but unfortunately is not so readily available.

# GUPPIES, MOLLIES, PLATIES & SWORDTAILS

As their name suggests, livebearers produce live young, rather than lay eggs, which is the typical method of reproduction among fish. These prolific fish are often among the first fish to breed in an aquarium; indeed, it is the main thing on a male's mind. So for the sake of the female, keep several females to every male so he splits his amorous advances equally, or only keep males. They are a varied group of fish, many of which are ideal candidates for a community tank. Their busy nature often takes them to all corners of the aquarium, which adds to their appeal. Livebearers are easy to keep and relatively undemanding in their needs, making them ideal beginner fish. As with all livebearers, the male can be distinguished by its gonopodium, a tubelike modification of the anal fin used in mating.

## Guppy ❤
### Poecilia reticulata

It is not hard to understand why the stunningly colorful and active guppy should be one of the all-time favorites of the community aquarium. The long flowing tails of the males have vibrant patterns in colors ranging from bright red to mottled green and yellow. Many guppy varieties have been bred to add to the naturally occurring color patterns. Selective breeding has also provided the fishkeeper with a range of tail shapes and sizes to choose from. As virtually all specimens offered for sale are farmed fish, the guppy, originally from Central America, is adapted to most aquarium environments. However, in soft water areas you may need to raise the hardness to ensure that the pH level does not drop too low. The peaceful guppies occupy the mid and upper layers of the tank and are ideal for the community aquarium, but avoid keeping them with boisterous barbs and Siamese fighting fish that will nip their flowing tails, leaving them stressed and very susceptible to disease.
Maximum adult size: 6 cm (2.4 in).

*The king cobra color form combines a beautifully mottled body with a banded tail.*

*The golden form glows in shades of yellow and orange.*

## Black Molly ❯
### *Poecilia sphenops*

The black molly is commonly available in aquarium shops and, although not as flamboyant as its sailfin cousin, it makes a lively addition to the middle and upper water levels of any community display. Its placid nature means that it will coexist happily with all other peaceful species. It must have hard water, with a pH of over 7.5. Maximum adult size: 6 cm (2.4 in).

*Male and female green sailfin mollies.*

## ▼ Sailfin Molly
### *Poecilia velifera*

The dorsal fin of the male sailfin molly is emblazoned with a multicolored mottled pattern and edged with gold. The pattern extends onto the tail and complements the scale pattern on each flank. The fish are usually sold in sexed pairs, and the male uses his magnificent dorsal fin to attract his female. Whilst the natural color of this Mexican fish is a green-yellow-silver mix, colored varieties are also available, including gold and silver. Mollies are active fish that patrol the middle to upper layers of the aquarium for food. The upturned mouth is characteristic of fish that feed from the surface in the wild, so floating flakes pose no problems in the aquarium. Despite its showy behavior, the sailfin molly is peaceful toward other tankmates, but for its own sake, do not keep it with potential fin-nippers. Keep mollies in hard water with a pH above 7.5. Maximum adult size: 15 cm (6 in).

*An elegant male orange sailfin molly.*

## Swordtail ▼

*Xiphophorus helleri*

The bright and colorful Central American swordtails bring a unique body shape to the community aquarium. Although the sword is only found on the males, females are just as brightly colored and usually larger than males. Swordtails are generally peaceful fish that appreciate the security of aquarium plants as they swim in the middle to upper water levels. If you are keeping more than one male, make sure there is plenty of cover, as they may become antagonistic toward each other. Swordtails are available in many color varieties. These have proved easy to develop, given the fishes' readiness to breed, which they will do in your aquarium. Maximum adult size: males (excluding sword) 10 cm (4 in), females 12 cm (4.7 in).

*Female pineapple swordtail*

*Male pineapple swordtail*

*Male green striped swordtail*

*Male red wag swordtail*

*This male of the black form is the swordtail version of the closely related tuxedo platy.*

## Platy ▼

*Xiphophorus maculatus*

The sociable and colorful
platy is ideally suited to the
community aquarium, although long-
finned varieties should not be kept with
boisterous barbs or Siamese fighting fish. Bear in
mind that platies may eat fine-leaved plants, although
broadleaved, larger plants will be safe from their
attentions. A worthy addition to any display, with
almost endless color varieties. Maximum adult size:
males 3.5 cm (1.4 in), females 6 cm (2.4 in).

*Male blue one-spot platy*

*Male orange platy*

*Female tuxedo platy*

*Male red
wagtail platy*

**Right:** *Two color
forms of platies
swim together in this
aquarium. The two
males at the top are
hi fin types, with a
larger dorsal fin than
normal forms. The
two females below
are sunset forms.*

During the following three weeks the aquarium will stabilize, ready to receive a third batch of more sensitive fish. ▶

# TOWARD A STABLE SYSTEM

After seven weeks the featured aquarium is making good progress. The plants have grown to cover the equipment on the lefthand side, and in time, the filter on the right will also be hidden from view. The plants are also filling the spaces left for them when they were first put in, and individuals of the same species, such as the hemianthus and cryptocoryne, now look like single specimens. A real sign that the plants are happy is that during the day they will photosynthesize so rapidly that they produce streams of oxygen bubbles from their leaves.

The plants are framing an open area toward the center of the aquarium, where we can view the fish as they play in the current created by the internal power filter. Their lively performance is proof that the effort made to provide them with a stable environment in these crucial early weeks has paid off; they are healthy, happy and thriving.

To keep the aquarium in good shape, it is time to consider some of the more long-term maintenance tasks that should become part of your regime. For example, the equipment you have installed will not run forever without some attention, and cleaning it must now be added to your list of regular tasks. Again, this is not difficult and does not take long, but is essential if the aquarium is to remain healthy and looking good.

If algae growth is proving to be a nuisance, it is vital to understand what stimulates it and how to eliminate it if possible. As water testing is the only way to gain a true insight into the aquatic habitat you are controlling, use the different tests available to explain any problems in the aquarium. For example, an excess of phosphate in the tap water supply might account for an unexpected algae bloom; the only way to confirm your suspicions is by carrying out a water test.

*It is now five weeks since the first fish were added and three weeks since the second fish went in. Most of the plants are thriving, but there is evidence of an algae problem. This is a critical time.*

## Algae spreads through the tank

High phosphate and nitrate levels plus excess light can boost algae growth. To solve the problem in this tank, the rate of water changes was increased for two weeks from one 10% change per week to two 10% changes per week. The water going back into the tank had less phosphate and nitrate in it. The lighting was reduced by half an hour at the beginning of the day. The algae soon died back, leaving a dusting of brown sludge that was removed. If husbandry changes are not enough, there are specific treatments suitable for use with aquarium plants. The better ones will alter the water chemistry, removing essential salts and preventing algae from growing. These changes have little or no effect on the plants in the aquarium.

**Above:** There is evidence of debris on this cryptocoryne leaf. It will be removed later on with the siphon gravel cleaner. Examine all the plants carefully for potential problems.

**Below:** Algae on the aquarium glass is not unusual. Algae problems can arise seemingly overnight, even in well-managed aquariums. Taking prompt action should keep them under control.

**Left:** Algae has also affected the Monosolenium tenerum at the front of the tank but this, too, can be removed by siphoning. It is vital to remove algae so that it cannot interfere with photosynthesis.

## Natural algae control

If you experience problems with excessive algae growth, even after reducing nitrate and phosphate levels, and treatments are not working effectively, there is a natural solution to the problem. While most algae-eating fish will only eat preferred types of algae, some shrimp from the *Caridina* family will eat almost all algae types, and the best species to use is the japonica shrimp *(Caridina multidentata)* also known as the algae shrimp or amano shrimp. This little creature will constantly remove algae from any surface, especially the leaves of plants and the substrate, without causing any damage to healthy plants. Along with the removal of algae, shrimp will also help to keep plant leaves free from debris, allowing the maximum amount of light to reach the plant. You will need a large group to get the best results; about 12–24 shrimp in a 60x30 cm (24x12 in) tank should keep algae completely at bay.

*Below: Not all snails are benign scavengers; the assassin snail actively hunts, kills and feeds on other small snails, making it an unusual but effective method of snail control.*

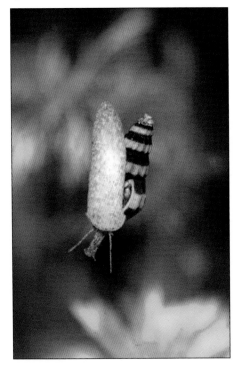

Because the shrimp are small, it is important to make sure that none of your fish are predatory and large enough to eat the shrimp, which would make a tasty snack. Shrimp can be sensitive to chemicals, so always check for warnings when using treatments in the aquarium, especially any that contain copper.

## Snail control

Along with algae, snails are another common and difficult pest in the aquarium. They can multiply rapidly, becoming unsightly and sometimes doing damage. Snails are almost impossible to avoid and usually arrive unseen on live plants, but in most cases they remain in low numbers and cause no harm. When the population of snails multiplies rapidly, the first thing to check is the quantity of food you are adding; the vast majority of snail problems are caused by leftover food in the aquarium.

Removing a large population of snails can be difficult and time-consuming. Snail-killing treatments are readily available but their effectiveness is limited and large

*Above: Adult japonica shrimp are well marked with a distinct yellow strip down the back, while younger specimens are virtually colorless. Several are needed to be effective.*

numbers of dead snails will cause water quality problems. You can use snail traps, but removing a significant proportion of snails by this method will take time.

One of the best methods of snail control is through natural predation and many scavenging fish species, such as bottom-dwelling loaches or catfish, will eat snails, but normally only the smaller ones. A slightly unusual, but very effective method of control, is to introduce a predatory snail species, the assassin snail, which will hunt down and kill other small snails. Assassin snails' main source of food is other snails, so they will steadily work their way through a tank until there are few visible snails left. Assassin snails do not reproduce as quickly as pest snails, and once their main food source is exhausted they will convert to scavenging and can be fed on sinking foods.

## CARE AND UPKEEP

As we have seen during the previous weeks, it is important to adopt a regular maintenance routine if the display is to look its best and the environment is to remain healthy. Before embarking on any maintenance, assemble all the equipment you will need, including a clean bucket for the water changes, sharp scissors for trimming plants and a bin for debris. Turn off the electricity supply. Leave yourself enough time to carry out the work slowly and carefully in order not to disturb the plants and substrate too much.

Clean the glass on a weekly basis. As time passes, the plants growing near the edges of the tank will require extra attention, otherwise they will grow too large and restrict easy access to the glass for cleaning. You may also need to move the substrate near the front of the aquarium to clear away any algae growing on the inside of the front glass below the substrate level. Do this very carefully to avoid damaging any plant roots. If in

***Above:*** *There is evidence of algae on the front glass. Wipe this away with a wad of filter wool and clean the remainder of the glass to give you a clear view of what is going on inside the tank.*

### Testing for phosphate

*Phosphate is present in tap water and is also gradually added to the aquarium via fish food. It can promote sudden unwanted algae growth and must be controlled to prevent the display from being ruined. After running for seven weeks, the featured tank has a high phosphate level of over 2.0ppm. This was suspected when the telltale signs of algae began to appear. Do not panic if this should happen; simply carry out water changes using water containing less phosphate to help reduce the overall level. A chemical resin filter media will rapidly reduce this level, starving the algae out of existence.*

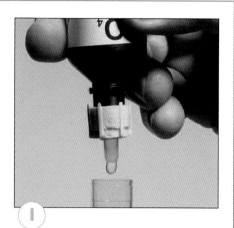

1  *Take a sample of water from the aquarium and slowly add eight drops of reagent from the yellow bottle.*

2  *Put the stopper on the test tube and shake the tube thoroughly. Leave the solution to develop for the recommended time.*

3  *Add two drops of reagent from the green bottle to the solution. Brands will vary in the numbers of bottles or drops for each step.*

4  *Shake the test tube again and allow it to stand as directed. Always follow the manufacturer's instructions exactly.*

5  *Remove the stopper and, looking down the tube from above, compare the color of the solution against the chart provided.*

doubt, you can leave the algae below the substrate level alone, otherwise you may do more harm than good.

Once you have had your hands in the water, you may need to wipe up drips on the outside of the aquarium. Only use aquarium glass cleaners, as they have been formulated to be safe with livestock. Most general household chemicals are toxic to fish and should not be used anywhere near the tank.

## Trimming the plants

As we discussed in week three (see page 104), it is necessary to prune the display plants to keep them in check and stop them from outgrowing their allotted space. It is also necessary to prune and remove older growth that starts to die off, as this will very quickly rot in the aquarium adding to the organic waste load on the biological filtration system. This is the case in the featured tank, where several of the leaves on the *Echinodorus* have started to become skeletal as the old tissue dies

*Below: Using sharp scissors, trim the leaf away cleanly at the base of the stalk and remove it from the aquarium. Plants will continue to look their best if you maintain them regularly.*

## Cleaning the CO2 pump

You will need to clean the small $CO_2$ dosing pump. The small bits of leaf from trimming the hemianthus have been sucked into the inlet; remove these with your fingers. Every two months take the pump out of the aquarium, rinse out the impeller and check for wear.

*Right: Plant trimmings may become lodged in the intake of the $CO_2$ water pump. Remove them with your fingers.*

*Left: Hemianthus will benefit from a regular "haircut" to encourage new, bushy growth and keep it tidy. One thorough trim is better than snipping away piecemeal every few days.*

*Right: As you trim the hemianthus, the ends will float off around the aquarium. Remove them with a fine net when you have finished cutting.*

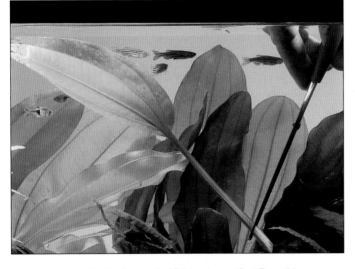

*Right: One leaf of Echinodorus "Red Flame" has completely died back and should be removed as soon as possible. It is unsightly and of no further use to the plant.*

**Above:** *In a water change, the aim is to replace 10%–20% of the water. This photo shows the water level after the siphoning shown opposite.*

**Right:** *Using a siphon cleaner, you can make a water change and remove algae and debris from plants, such as Monosolenium, at the same time.*

and starts to decay. Be sure to trim these stems as near as possible to the crown of the plant, leaving very little to rot in the aquarium. Carry out this task on a regular basis.

## Water changes

In week three we began a program of water changes to dilute the constant production of nitrate. After the influx of algae in the aquarium, we were left with a residue of dead algae amongst the plant leaves and on the substrate. Again, it is vital to remove this dead matter to prevent it rotting down in the aquarium, and the best tool for this job is a siphon-action gravel cleaner. Here we look more closely at using this device and making a water change at the same time.

Most good models have a built-in, self-start priming mechanism so there is no need for you to suck on the end of a hose

and risk taking in a mouthful of aquarium water. The broad tube and wide foot allow you to vacuum a large area of the tank, as you siphon out the water into a bucket. Guide the foot gently over the plant leaves to remove the fine dusting of dead algae and also into the top of the substrate. This will be sucked up into the tube of the gravel cleaner and whirled round in the water flow to separate it from any debris. The heavier substrate particles then sink back down to the floor of the aquarium, and the slightly more buoyant silt is sucked out and into the bucket. Repeat this process over the entire display, but make sure you do not remove more than a total of 25% of the aquarium water in the course of the cleaning operation. Do not worry if you do not manage to vacuum the whole tank; just remember to tackle the parts you missed the following week. As the bucket fills up with water from the

**Below:** Guide the siphon cleaner from one side of the aquarium to the other. It will remove organic debris in the substrate, as well as any waste matter disturbed while you trimmed the plants.

**Right:** Continue to siphon out the water and clean the plants and gravel until you have removed as much algae and debris as possible and the water is at the desired level. Do not siphon out any fish!

A flexible hose attached to the siphon takes water from the aquarium.

**Right:** Direct the water from the tank into a bucket on the ground. Siphon cleaners operate on the basis of removing lighter wastes while leaving the substrate relatively intact.

aquarium, stop the siphoning and empty it. Then restart the siphon as before. Do not discard the last bucket of water taken from the aquarium as you will need it for the next maintenance stage: the essential task of filter cleaning.

## Cleaning the internal filter

Any filtration system, whether it be an external canister, hang-on or the internal filter used in this aquarium, needs regular maintenance if it is to function properly and have a long life.

Start by dismantling the filter and clean each part as illustrated on the following pages. Place the pieces in the bucket and rinse them in the old aquarium water, using a small piece of filter wool to remove stubborn debris.

The only moving part in this unit is the impeller that spins to pump the water. Clean it and check it for wear and tear. If it shows any sign of damage after a few months, be sure to replace it, as a worn, off-center impeller will undermine the motor head and render the unit useless. Impellers are a readily available spare part from your aquatic store.

The last part to be cleaned, because it is the dirtiest, is the biological filter medium. In the case of this tank, the filter medium is the blue foam, which also traps solid debris from the aquarium. Gently squeezing the foam in the bucket of old aquarium water will release nearly all the solid debris. The most important thing to remember at this stage is that the filter medium supports the vital *Nitrosomonas* and *Nitrobacter* bacteria on which the fishes' lives depend. NEVER wash any filter media in tap water, which contains chlorine and chloramine that will kill the beneficial bacteria in the filter media (see page 92 for more details).

When all the parts of the filter are clean, reassemble the unit and return it to the aquarium. Remember to turn on the electricity, and make sure that all the systems are working properly. The filter will probably need cleaning every month.

**Above:** *Before carrying out any maintenance work on the tank, always switch off the electricity supply and, to be on the safe side, unplug it as well. Then start by removing the filter from its cradle.*

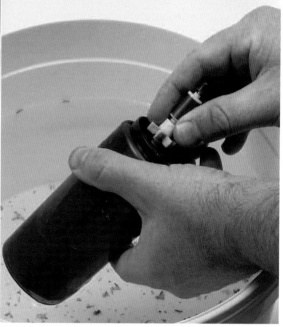

**Right:** *Working over the bucket of water that you siphoned out of the tank, remove the impeller and put it in the water. Stand the filter in the bucket while you work on each component.*

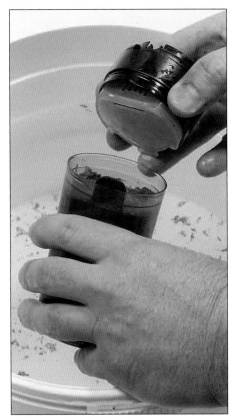

**Above:** Open up the casing that houses the filter media. Internal filters need cleaning every four to six weeks. If you wear rubber gloves, choose ones that allow you to use your hands freely.

**Above:** Remove the filter foam from the casing and put it in the bucket. Using water from the aquarium means you will not destroy the bacteria that have accumulated in the sponge.

**Above:** Wipe out the casing with filter wool dipped in aquarium water. When it is clean you can see through it more clearly so that you can monitor the state of the filter foam inside.

**Above and right:** Using fresh filter wool if necessary, wipe the casing inside and out, taking care to remove any plant fragments that have become trapped in the narrow slots.

**Above:** *Clean the insert plate that holds the media in the filter. Because the aquarium relies so heavily on the efficiency of the filter, it is worth cleaning each element as thoroughly as possible.*

**Above:** *Clean off any slime that has accumulated on the impeller and the shaft, as well as in the housing. Take this opportunity to check whether the bearings need replacing.*

## Activated carbon

Activated carbon is a very useful and widely available filter medium. It will remove chemicals, toxins and organic wastes by absorbing them onto active sites on its surface. It can be prepared from a number of sources, and these give the carbon different characteristics. Using a blended product is the best strategy. It should be housed in a separate chamber in the filter or contained in a filter media bag. This is because it will have to be removed if disease treatments are used in the aquarium. Replace the activated carbon every four to six weeks, in line with the maker's instructions.

**Below:** *If the filter has a separate media compartment, you can use it for activated carbon. Before refilling it, clean the inside and rinse out the foam pad at the bottom.*

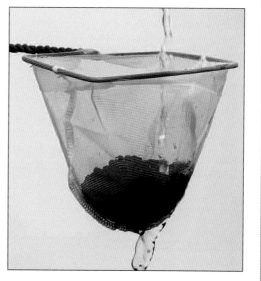

**Above:** *Before use, rinse new batches of activated carbon in a fine net held under running tap water. This will flush out any carbon dust and small particles that would otherwise cloud the aquarium.*

**Below and right:** *Remove the foam from the canister and squeeze it out in the aquarium water in the bucket to retain the colony of beneficial bacteria. Remove any visible debris.*

**Below:** *By the time you have finished, the filter foam will look a lot cleaner. It is a good idea to replace the filter foam when it shows signs of not returning to its original shape when squeezed.*

*When renewing filter foam, cut the old and new pieces in half. Run the new and old halves together for a month to allow the new filter foam to become seeded with the nitrifying bacteria.*

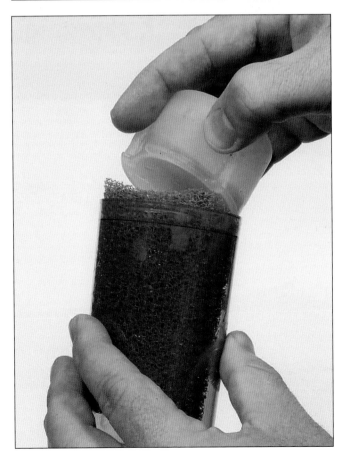

**Left:** *Reassemble the filter in the reverse order of dismantling it. Ensure the foam sits properly in the canister as water will take any opportunity to bypass it, making the filter inefficient.*

**Right:** *With the impeller in place, fit the water pump securely on top of the canister. Replace the unit in the tank and ensure that it floods fully. Any air trapped inside will stop the filter working properly.*

*Do not allow the filter medium to dry out during cleaning. Return the unit to the tank as soon as possible.*

You can take advantage of the lower water level to carry out some more serious plant maintenance. In the righthand corner of this aquarium, the *Echinodorus* "Red Special" and *Cryptocoryne wendtii* "Tropica" have grown vigorously and are overshadowing the *Glossostigma* in the foreground, even though we left room for all the plants to develop. Without sufficient light, the *Glossostigma* will suffer. To prevent permanent damage to it, there are two options: either prune back the taller midground plant or move the foreground one. Start by examining the midground plant. Will pruning it give it an unnatural appearance? If so, then moving

the foreground plant is the best option. On this occasion, we have decided to move the foreground plant. First identify where it is to go. Do this before you put your hands in the tank so that you can see where the light penetrates to the base of the aquarium. Once you have identified the new planting position, cradle your fingers and push them very gently into the substrate all the way around the base of the plant. Slowly lift the plant free of the substrate. Replant it with your hand in the same cradle position and coax the substrate around the base of the plant. Once in its new position, it will start to flourish after a couple of weeks.

## Refilling the tank

When all the maintenance is complete, refill the tank. Cold tap water may cause a temperature shock so warm it up first, either by leaving it to stand for 24 hours or by mixing in a small amount of boiling water to achieve a temperature similar to the main tank. Never use warm tap water, as this can contain harmful heavy metals from your heating system. Add a tap water conditioner (see page 90). When this has been thoroughly incorporated, pour the water into the aquarium using a jug. It is not a good idea to pour the water straight from a bucket, as it is heavy and difficult to control.

**1** This glossostigma has become overshadowed by the plants around it and needs to be moved forward.

**2** Holding the rootball, loosen the substrate around the plant and lift it out gently. Try not to damage the delicate roots.

**3** Identify the new planting position and make a dip in the substrate with one finger. Bury the plant roots in the hole.

**4** Bank up the substrate around the plant and firm it in. It is important to monitor the progress of all the plants in the aquarium, especially the smaller varieties.

**5** In its new, brighter position, the glossostigma should make good progress. A living aquarium is a changing environment and adjustments like this help to keep it looking its best.

## Giving overshadowed plants a chance

*Left:* Having moved one Glossostigma elatinoides, look at the others to see how they are progressing.

This one at the righthand side of the aquarium is also overshadowed.

*Left:* Once relocated, this plant is in a much better position. In the right conditions, the three plants will soon grow together.

*Left:* When all the maintenance has been completed, refill the tank with water that has been conditioned as described on page 92. Even small amounts of untreated tap water are harmful to fish.

*Above:* Pour the conditioned water slowly into the aquarium to avoid disturbing the plants and substrate. Ideally, it should be at or near the same temperature as the water in the tank.

# FEEDING PLANTS

Like all living organisms, plants need food in order to grow and remain healthy. The nutrients they require are usually described as macro- or micronutrients. Macronutrients are required in greater quantities than micronutrients, but both are equally important to the plant's survival. Macronutrients are mainly responsible for building the structure of plants while micronutrients are used in biochemical processes within plant cells. The roles these nutrients play are listed in the panels on these pages.

## Sources of nutrients

Tap water is usually well supplied with several of the macro- and micronutrients

### Essential micronutrients

**Boron** is used in many processes, including flower and root production.

**Chlorine** is required in minute quantities for biochemical processes, including photosynthesis.

**Copper** is used by enzymes involved in respiration.

**Iron** is a vital trace nutrient required for chlorophyll synthesis, enzyme production and respiration.

**Manganese** activates enzymes in chlorophyll production and photosynthesis.

**Molybdenum** is used in an enzyme to break down nitrate into useful ammonium for building proteins.

**Nickel** is used in very small amounts for an enzyme that converts urea to ammonia.

**Zinc** is used for chlorophyll production. Only required in tiny amounts.

**Right:** *Pour a measured dose of fertilizer into the water. Do not be tempted to add more than directed. Over-fertilization can be just as harmful as not feeding enough.*

**Below:** *Good-quality liquid fertilizers can provide a valuable source of iron and other essential nutrients to aquarium plants. Use them regularly, usually every one or two weeks.*

required by plants. Indeed, sometimes they are present to excess, as in the case of phosphate. Generally speaking, if you carry out routine partial water changes, you can be confident that your aquarium plants will receive a regular supply of the nutrients they need. A proprietary liquid fertilizer will supply and/or supplement any shortfall.

Nitrogen is available to plants both from tap water and in the form of nitrate, the end product of the ongoing nitrogen cycle (see page 92). Plants can also absorb ammonium from the water as a source of nitrogen.

Terrestrial plants obtain their supply of carbon from the carbon dioxide gas ($CO_2$) in the air, but submerged aquatic plants rely on carbon dioxide dissolved in the water. This is never available in sufficient quantities in an aquarium for plants to grow and remain healthy, and so levels must be boosted by the aquarist for vigorous displays. Without sufficient $CO_2$, the amount of photosynthetic activity required for the plant to thrive cannot be achieved. The carbon dioxide dosing system installed in the aquarium during the initial setup (page 26) will provide the required level of $CO_2$ for this display.

The laterite mixed into the substrate when the aquarium was assembled, along with fertilizers and organic waste, will form a major food store for the plants. The reddish color of the laterite indicates the presence of iron, which is vital for healthy plant growth. The laterite will nourish the plants during the first year. Thereafter, additional fertilization is needed to meet their nutritional needs.

Plants can most easily absorb iron in the "smaller" bivalent form ($Fe^{2+}$) and this will be the form that aquarium fertilizers supply. Iron is one of several metal-based micronutrients that can be "lost" to plants in an aquarium by being oxidized into another form (in this case, $Fe^{3+}$) that plants find difficult to take up. In order for iron, for example, to remain continually available to aquarium plants, it should be supplied in a chelated form. Chelates are organic compounds that bind to iron and prevent it from being converted to the form that cannot be taken up. A good substrate will hold nutrients in a chelated form over long periods.

Although liquid fertilizers generally provide many of the required micronutrients, they do not supply the major macronutrients. (Adding extra doses of nitrate and phosphate will only encourage unwanted algae.) Most liquid fertilizers should be supplied every seven to fourteen days, as the nutrients are quickly used up by the aquarium plants.

Tablet fertilizers are an alternative to liquid products. Unlike liquid feeds, which blanket feed the whole aquarium, you can use tablets to feed particular plants. They are also ideal for feeding plants once the laterite in the substrate is exhausted after the first year. Tablets are usually packed full of iron and other trace elements and release their nutrients slowly. Always follow the manufacturer's dosage instructions. They are easy to use; simply push them into the substrate near the roots of each plant you wish to feed.

The final source of plant nutrition comes, perhaps unexpectedly, from fish foods. They are usually rich in both potassium and phosphate, and waste passed by fish feeding on the foods will provide plants with a steady supply of these nutrients. There is no way of accurately dosing the nutrients supplied in this way, but in an aquarium well stocked with fish this can be a good way of feeding the aquarium plants.

Uneaten fish food can also feed plants, as bacteria break down the leftover fragments and release the nutrients they contain. Unfortunately, leftover food will also pollute the aquarium and provide ideal conditions for harmful fungal and bacterial diseases to thrive, so it should be avoided at all costs.

## Essential macronutrients

**Calcium** is used in cell wall structure.

**Carbon** is used as a major building block of plants — in fact, of all living organisms.

**Magnesium** is a vital component of chlorophyll and is needed to activate vital enzymes involved in biological processes.

**Nitrogen**, mainly in the form of ammonium, is used to build up proteins.

**Oxygen** is used in cell wall structure and for respiration to release energy from food. It is the major by-product of photosynthesis.

**Phosphorus** is essential for healthy root formation and flower production. It also plays an important role in energy transfer processes within the plant.

**Potassium** is vital for key biological functions in growth and reproduction.

**Sulphur** is required for producing proteins and the photosynthetic pigment chlorophyll.

## Adding a tablet fertilizer

**1**

*Tablet fertilizers supply nutrients directly to the roots. "Greedy" plants that need plenty of iron will benefit from this method of fertilization.*

**2**

*Tablet fertilizers are supplied in blister packs. Pop one tablet out of the pack and place it on the substrate near the roots of the plant.*

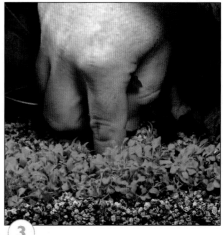

**3**

*Push the tablet into the substrate under or close to the roots so that they can easily absorb the essential nutrients as the tablet breaks down.*

## ADDING THIRD FISH

The final group of fish to be added to the aquarium are species that have more specific needs than the first two groups.

The pair of elegant cockatoo cichlids (*Apistogramma cacatuoides*) will form a lasting bond in the aquarium and may even breed. Their breeding behavior involves setting up a territory to protect their young and to do this they will bully the other inhabitants. Making sure fish like these have plenty of space and suitable territory will help them fit in more sociably with other fish.

We are also adding some otocinclus catfish at this stage. They carry out a very important housekeeping role in the aquarium by eating algae. Ideally, there should be some algae for them to eat. Even though we try to create algae-free conditions, it is hard not to have an ongoing population somewhere in the aquarium. If algae are in very short supply, the otocinclus will soon learn to feed on the algae wafers fed to the other catfish.

**Above:** *Now that the water conditions have stabilized, it is safe to add the third batch of fish. These are otocinclus catfish. Float the plastic bag in the aquarium for about 20 minutes.*

**Below:** *A pair of colorful cockatoo cichlids* (Apistogramma cacatuoides) *waiting to be released from their plastic bag. Ideally, quarantine new fish to safeguard your existing population.*

**Above:** *When the water temperatures in the bag and in the aquarium have equalized, you can release the fish. Always check that there are no fish left in the bag before you dispose of it.*

**Above:** *Upend the bag just above the water surface and allow the fish to swim out. Do not tip them into the tank from a great height. This aquarium will house a group of otocinclus catfish.*

**Right:** *Unlike some of the cichlids, cockatoo cichlids (this is a male) can be safely housed in a planted aquarium. At 8 cm (3.2 in), they do not grow too large and will use the plants to establish territories. They may even breed.*

**Left:** *This newly released otocinclus has settled on a plant leaf. Being algae-eaters, these busy little catfish will have a valuable role to play in the aquarium, browsing constantly on plants and the tank glass.*

# THIRD FISH

The third and final group of fish to add to the aquarium will generate the real "wow" factor. They are best left until last, either because they require the security provided by established plants or because they are somewhat territorial. If added last, they will not regard the tank as their exclusive territory and try to chase off other fish added after them. These fish will probably be the most expensive ones you buy, so it pays to introduce them into a mature, stable environment that has been running successfully for several weeks.

*Female*

*Male*

*The longer dorsal fin of the male black phantom tetra is clear, even in these young fish. The female (top fish) has reddish pelvic fins and does not develop such a large dorsal fin.*

## Black Phantom Tetra ▲
*Megalamphodus megalopterus*

The beauty of this small tetra from Brazil lies in its silky black markings that put it in a class of its own. It is the complete opposite of the vivid neons and cardinals, and the "silent" colors speak loudly when these shoaling fish are contrasted against their brighter cousins in the display. Although a firm favorite in many aquariums, it is not the easiest tetra to keep. Good water quality, including low nitrate levels, must be maintained if it is to thrive. In good conditions, the males may exhibit breeding behavior and have mock fights. This should not be confused with bullying and is usually harmless to the individuals involved. Do not keep black phantom tetras with larger, potentially aggressive fish. Maximum adult size: 4.5 cm (1.8 in).

## Rummy Nose Tetra ❯
*Hemigrammus bleheri*

The rummy nose, from Colombia and Brazil, is one of Nature's little stunners and a real gem for any aquarium. Its black-and-white striped tail and silver body with a bright red marking running from the nose to behind the eye look as if they had been painted by a child. Its sleek, torpedolike body is suited to life in fast-flowing streams and the rummy nose will enjoy playing in the flow return from the filter. Pay particular attention to water quality; even high nitrate levels will cause this delicate tetra to suffer. The rummy nose does best in a well-planted aquarium where the water quality is at its best and there is ample cover. A minimum of eight individuals will make a good display. Avoid keeping them with larger, potentially aggressive fish. Maximum adult size: 4.5 cm (1.8 in).

## ▲ Red Phantom Tetra

*Megalamphodus sweglesi*

The red phantom tetra from Colombia is a close cousin of the black phantom, featuring similar black markings but on a red background. It is even more delicate than the black phantom and requires very good conditions to do well. However, the effort is worthwhile, as the fish will reward you with its stunning red hues and placid behavior. The red phantom should be one of the last fish you add to your display, as all the aquarium conditions need to be as stable as possible before you introduce it. The red phantom looks best in a small shoal of six to eight individuals. Avoid keeping it with larger, potentially aggressive fish. Maximum adult size: 4.5 cm (1.8 in).

# Cichlids

The cichlids in your aquarium will form the real "personalities" in the display. They are some of the most colorful fish you can choose, but restrict yourself to a pair from a single species for all but the largest of community displays. Males and females are usually very different in many ways — color, body shape, size — and this adds to the attraction of this group of fish.

In a healthy, well-maintained aquarium, many of the cichlid species on these pages will readily spawn and produce large quantities of fry. Some of the young will be predated on by the other fish, as would happen in the wild. Only a few healthy and lucky fish will grow to adulthood, but this all adds to the excitement of fishkeeping. Should your cichlids spawn they will defend an area of the tank as their own, but as long as there is plenty of foliage for the other fish to hide in, and the cichlids are not housed with overly slow species, then all the tank's inhabitants should have room to coexist. All of the cichlids described here should be kept with peaceful species only.

### Laetacara dorsiger ▶

These lovely round-faced cichlids from Bolivia and Rio Paraguay bring welcome color into the aquarium. Their red bellies, with hints of blue when the males and females are breeding, show off the fish well. Both the male and female have a characteristic black spot on the dorsal fin, but the male's dorsal fin is much more developed. Like most small cichlids, they will be busy around the aquarium and have a huge appetite. They prefer some form of cover in the display, such as bogwood or rocks. This little cichlid is very peaceful, even when spawning, so it makes an ideal fish for any community display. Do not confuse this species with Laetacara curviceps, whose aggressive nature during breeding makes it unsuitable for the community aquarium. Maximum adult size: 6–8 cm (2.4–3.2 in).

### Keyhole Cichlid
*Aequidens maronii*

Because this small, peaceful Guyanan fish mixes well with most other species, it is one of the most commonly kept community aquarium cichlids. The distinctive "keyhole" marking on each flank is vivid black when the fish is happy, but in stressed fish the color of the flank fades to a murky brown all over. Keyholes also have a black line running through the eye down each flank to the edge of the gill cover. These cichlids thrive best when kept in pairs, and will lovingly care for their fry for a few months before allowing them to fend for themselves. The fish will benefit from relatively dense planting to provide cover in the aquarium, which they use for their own security. Maximum adult size: 10–12 cm (4–4.7 in).

### ▼ Agassiz's Dwarf Cichlid
*Apistogramma agassizii*

This small, but stunningly elegant, Amazonian cichlid makes up in color for what it lacks in size. The beautiful golden-red back and dorsal fin are in complete contrast to the grayish blue-green flanks and tail. The blue coloration also spreads in a marbled pattern onto each side of the head, making this fish a real gem. Males are generally larger than females and have a more pointed tail. As it is usually quite easy to identify the sexes, these fish are often sold in pairs. However, if they are to breed, you will need to house one male with several females. Being so small, Agassiz's cichlid appreciates the cover provided by dense planting and root-shaped pieces of bogwood. Maximum adult size: 8 cm (3.2 in).

## Viejita Dwarf ▲ Cichlid

*Apistogramma viejita*

In this colorful little South American cichlid species, the male's bright yellow breeding color is simply stunning. He is much larger than the female, with elongated fins and black spots along the back and flanks. These fish may spawn in your aquarium and will take over a cave in order to do so. They will defend this from the other inhabitants in the aquarium, but only if they approach too close to the eggs or fry. *A. viejita* will thrive on a good-quality flake food. Maximum adult size: Males 7.5 cm (3 in), females 3–4 cm (1.2–1.6 in).

## Borelli's Dwarf Cichlid ❯

*Apistogramma borelli*

The flowing fins of this elegant small cichlid often look a bit big for its body! They carry the grayish blue-green and gold colors from the body and create a wonderful display. The males are half as big again as the females and have pointed dorsal and anal fins. These South American cichlids like to spend time amongst leaves in the upper layers of the aquarium, so include taller plant species in your display. Maximum adult size: Males 8 cm (3.2 in), females 4–5 cm (1.6–2 in).

## Checkerboard Cichlid ▶

*Dicrossus filamentosus*

The small, delicate stature of this superb South American cichlid makes it suitable for even the smallest aquarium display. The checkerboard spots along each flank are bordered by two light blue lines that end on the pointed tail. The male's fins turn red as he enters breeding condition, while those of the female remain transparent. Both sexes enjoy the cover of a densely planted aquarium. If a pair should spawn they will defend the nest, but most other fish will be able to keep out of their way. The checkerboard cichlid will fit in with the majority of community fish, but avoid keeping it with other cichlids. Maximum adult size: Males 9 cm (3.5 in), females up to 6 cm (2.4 in).

## ▼ Cockatoo Cichlid

*Apistogramma cacatuoides*

Both the male and female cockatoo cichlid from the Amazon have stunning coloration, which makes them striking show fish and worth considering for any community aquarium display. The male sports a huge, pointed dorsal fin, patterned with red, orange and yellow, hence the fish's common name. The smaller female contributes just as much to the display, being bright yellow with a jet black line along each flank. Despite her smaller size, the female can be the more adventurous fish as she moves around the aquarium. The cockatoo cichlid is difficult to breed, as males prefer to have several females in the aquarium, which can ruin the balance of your display. However, a single female may choose a breeding cave amongst rocks and wood in the aquarium and the male may succumb to her charms. Avoid keeping with other cichlids, unless they are in a large aquarium. Maximum adult size: Males up to 9 cm (3.5 in), females up to 5 cm (2 in).

## Kribensis ▼

*Pelvicachromis pulcher*

The krib, from Nigeria, is the community cichlid most commonly found in aquarium shops. This popularity is easily explained by the fish's spectacular colors. The head is often striped black-and-yellow, while the underside has a vibrant red glow. As with all small cichlids, the colors become even more marked if the conditions are suitable for breeding and the fish start to court. Males can be identified by their pointed dorsal fin and they also tend to be larger than the females. This is one species that will readily breed in the aquarium. The female lays her eggs on the roof of a cave or on any flat surface. The fry hatch within a few days and will be guarded by the parents until they are old enough to forage for food by themselves. To give the fry a good start in life, feed them with a liquid fry food. This will supply all their needs until they can take solid fry food. Only keep one pair of adults per aquarium. Maximum adult size: 8–10 cm (3.2–4 in).

*Female ram*

## ▲ Striped Dwarf Cichlid

*Pelvicachromis taeniatus*

Although similar to the kribensis, *P. taeniatus*, from Nigeria and Cameroon, is usually more yellow in color. However, this species can have many different color variants, depending on where the original wild-caught specimens came from. The red body spot can range from yellow-red through pink to purple. A common feature on most color variants is a gold tail with black spots. *P. taeniatus* will take advantage of plant cover in order to feel secure, but does benefit from a generous space in which to swim around freely. Although these cichlids can be bred in the aquarium, they are more difficult to raise than kribensis, as the fry are harder to feed. However, this should not deter you from keeping these vibrant little cichlids. Keep in slightly acid water. Maximum adult size: 7–9 cm (2.75–3.5 in).

*Male ram*

## ▲ Ram, or Butterfly Cichlid

*Microgeophagus ramirezi*

The ram's bright blue, reticulated scales create a stunning backdrop for the black, white and gold patterns toward the head of both the male and female. These stunning colors are set off by a red outline to both the top and bottom of the tail. Several color forms are available. The relatively small size and very peaceful nature of the Ram, which comes from Venezuela and Colombia, make it ideal for the smaller community display. Prefers some plant cover. Maximum adult size: 7 cm (2.75 in).

### Nanochromis parilus ❯

Although it will venture up to midwater level, especially when food is on offer, this subtly colored small cichlid is very much at home in the lower reaches, where it enjoys scooting around the bottom of aquarium. The elongated body adds a different shape to the display. It is yellow-brown in color, with a blue-and-red underside. The tail and dorsal fin are brightly marked with stripes and dashes to rival any nation's flag design. These cichlids from Zaire are best suited to the larger display, as males (top fish) can be a little territorial. An aquarium with plenty of plants and decor will provide cover, both for the cichlid and its tankmates. Maximum adult size: 7–8 cm (2.75–3.2 in).

## Small cichlids to avoid

The following common cichlid species should not be included in the average community display as they have a tendency to be too territorial and therefore aggressive toward their tankmates. This does not mean that you should always avoid these fish, as many make excellent aquarium subjects. They do, however, require a more specific setup tailored to their needs. In addition to considering this shortlist, you should always take advice from your retailer regarding the suitability of any fish.

Convict cichlid (*Cichlasoma nigrofasciatum*)
Crown jewel cichlid (*Hemichromis cristatus*)
Firemouth cichlid (*Thorichthys meeki*)
Green terror (*Aequidens rivulatus*)
Port acara (*Aequidens portalegrensis*)
Red devil (*Amphilophus labiatus*)
Texas cichlid (*Herichthys cyanoguttatus*)

## Nijsseni's Dwarf ❯ Cichlid

*Apistogramma nijsseni*
This attractive fish from Peru is one of the best dwarf cichlids you can buy for your aquarium. It is an ideal community fish as it is rarely territorial. The male and female have very different but equally vibrant colors. The male has cobalt blue flanks, with a gold belly and pelvic fins, plus a red-rimmed tail. The bright gold female is much smaller, with black markings. Both fish need a well-planted tank to feel secure. Breeding them is difficult, but if the conditions suit the fish, they could well spawn in your display. Maximum adult size: males 4–6.5 cm.

# Angelfish ❯
## *Pterophyllum scalare*

Angelfish have been a firm favorite with fishkeepers for generations. Their extended dorsal and anal fins create a diamond shape that is unique in the aquarium. In recent years, hobbyists and commercial farmers worldwide have bred many color morphs, but all with the same distinctive body shape. The fish originate from the Amazon River, but the natural color — silver body with black vertical stripes — is rarely seen, even though it is one of the most stunning combinations. The deep-bodied altum angels *(Pterophyllum altum)* look fantastic when kept in a shoal and have more vivid markings than their more commonly seen cousins but they are much more demanding of soft/acid water. Angelfish have a reputation for picking off small tankmates, especially neon and cardinal tetras. Therefore, you should only keep them with peaceful community fish (other than small tetras) that are more than 3 cm (1.2 in) long. Angelfish will breed, but only in soft, acidic water maintained to the highest standards. Maximum adult size: 15 cm (6 in). (Altum angels up to 38 cm/15 in tall and 25 cm/10 in long.)

Angelfish
(Pterophyllum
scalare)

Altum
angelfish
(Pterophyllum
altum)

# CATFISH

### Clown Plec ▶
*Peckoltia vittata*

This is the ideal suckermouth catfish for all but the smallest of displays and beginners will find it easy to cater to. It will happily browse on any algae growing on plant leaves and decor. In addition to tablet and wafer foods, it will relish the treat of a chunk of cucumber weighted down in the tank. The yellow-gold striped pattern adds another dimension to the display. In common with other suckermouth catfish, it appreciates somewhere to hide. Maximum adult size: 10 cm (4 in).

### Bristlenose Ancistrus ▼
*Ancistrus temminckii*

The bristlenose ancistrus is a superb example of a suckermouth catfish. The head and body have a mottled brown-and-yellow pattern all over. However, it is the bristles on the nose that are so distinctive. They help this bottom-dwelling fish find its way around in the dark or when water visibility is poor, and are a wonderful example of the diverse body shapes that can add interest to your display. Bristlenoses often hop around on the aquarium decor, rasping any algae growth from rocks and wood. Provide them with some hiding places. Maximum adult size: 12 cm (4.7 in).

## *Peckoltia* L134 ▶

This stunning little catfish from South America is one of many species available to the aquarium trade that has not yet been scientifically named, hence the "L" number. It will thrive in a community setup, but can be a little territorial toward other catfish around its favorite hiding place. Like some other small catfish, it is omnivorous and will prefer a mixture of bloodworm and algae wafers in its diet. Check with your retailer about the water conditions it has been kept in; the pH should be no higher than 7.4. This wonderful little catfish grows to 11 cm (4.3 in). Provide an aquascape containing rocks and wood for this suckermouth catfish to hang around on.

## ▲ Starry Bristlenose Ancistrus

*Ancistrus* sp. L59 "White Seam"
Starry white spots on black skin, plus white-edged dorsal and caudal fins combine to produce a truly distinctive fish. The peaceful nature of this bottom-dwelling Ancistrus is another reason why this little gem of a catfish is ideal for the community tank. Make sure it has some hiding places to which it can retreat from the brightest lights. This ancistrus prefers water on the slightly acidic side, but your retailer may stock some fish acclimatized to your local water conditions. Maximum adult size: 8 cm (3.2 in).

## Glass Catfish
*Kryptopterus bicirrhis*

The almost translucent body of the aptly named glass catfish makes this an interesting and unusual Southeast Asian species. The backbone and supporting bones are clearly visible as it swims peacefully in the midwater level of the aquarium. Long barbels are another defining feature. Provide some cover with dense planting and keep in groups of six to eight.. Maximum adult size: 9 cm (3.5 in).

## Dwarf Otocinclus
*Otocinclus affinis*

If your aquarium ever experiences unwanted algae growth, then the *Otocinclus* species are Nature's solution to the problem. Perched on even the smallest plant leaves or up against the glass, they rasp on the algae, keeping it under control at all levels in the tank. Given this constant browsing behavior, it is important to observe the fish carefully and provide a supply of algae tablets and wafers when natural levels get low. These tiny fish are suited to displays of all sizes. Maximum adult size: 4 cm (1.6 in).

The popular, algae-eating *Otocinclus* species, of which *O. vittatus* is another example, are much better suited to a display than the traditional algae loach (*Gyrinocheilus aymonieri*), which usually eats plants as well as algae, and grows aggressive in the aquarium. The placid *Otocinclus*, on the other hand, minds it own business and grazes the entire aquarium of any algae (except blue-green, brown and brush), on whatever it may be growing. Other *Otocinclus* species are available and all require the same care. This means offering additional supplies of processed algae foods when natural levels are reduced. Maximum adult size: 4.5 cm (1.8 in).

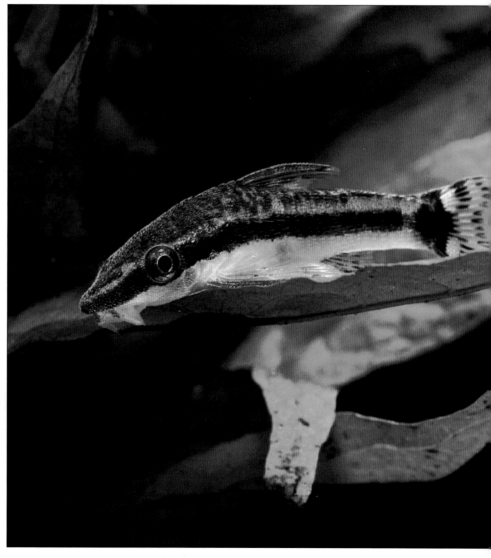

### ◀ **Upside-Down Catfish**
#### *Synodontis nigriventris*

As its common name suggests, the upside-down catfish spends a lot of its time in this position. Because its mouth, as with other catfish in its family, faces downward, it must turn upside-down to feed effectively. In the aquarium the fish should be given objects which they can easily sit beneath, such as wood, roots or large-leaved plants. The fish are peaceful and do not grow as large as some synodontis catfish, but they may still eat very small fish. Maximum adult size: 12 cm (5 in).

*In its wild environment, the fish browses the underside of leaves, wood and the water surface for small bugs and other food.*

### **Twig Catfish** ▼
#### *Farlowella vittata*

The twig catfish from Brazil is an unusual addition to the aquarium. This "stick insect" of the fish world looks streamlined and elegant perched on a stone, leaf or root, but its swimming action is somewhat ungainly. This is partly due to its body shape, but its movement is also restricted by protective armor-plated scales and it never swims far. These peaceful fish occupy the bottom level and prefer a tank interior with some hiding places, where they can avoid the more boisterous members of the display. So that they can feed in relative peace, offer them algae tablets and wafers in an area of the tank away from where the other fish are feeding on flake food. Maximum adult size: 15 cm (6 in).

## Whiptail Catfish ▼

*Sturisoma aureum*

The whiptail catfish holds its pectoral and dorsal fins erect for most of the time. It is easily recognized by the broad, dark stripe running along the body from the nose to the evenly forked tail. The tip of the nose is slightly upturned, while the mouth is on the underside, halfway between the nose and the eyes. The fish is a rampant algae browser, controlling most unwanted growths to the extent that it will need dietary supplements in the form of algae tablets and wafers. The whiptail, from Colombia, is a peaceful fish that occupies the bottom and middle levels of the tank. If you direct the flow from the power filter so that it passes directly over an exposed piece of wood or rock, the fish will happily sit there. *S. aureum* is ideal for any aquarium over 50 cm (20 in) long.

Maximum adult size: 15 cm (6 in).

### ◀ Zebra otocinclus

*Otocinclus cocama*

Zebra otocinclus is a relative newcomer to the fishkeeping hobby, only becoming available in 2001. In common with all the otocinclus, it must be kept in groups of at least five or six. The fish will constantly forage among the plants removing algae. Indeed, they are so efficient at removing algae that they should be offered algal wafers, lettuce or zucchini to keep them well fed. They must have a mature aquarium and stable water quality, so these little fish should be later additions to your tank. Maximum size 4–4.5 cm (1.6–1.8 in).

## LOACHES

### Horse-Face Loach ▼

*Acanthopsis choirorhynchus*

This unique member of the carp family is a joy to keep. The horse-face loach is a long, thin fish that rummages beneath the surface of the substrate looking for food. This habit makes the fish a perfect ally for the fishkeeper, as it keeps the substrate clean and prevents it stagnating and becoming compacted. Often, the horse-face loach buries into the substrate, leaving only its head showing, while all the other fish swim around oblivious to it. However, it is important to provide a substrate with no sharp edges on which the fish could damage itself. The horse-face loach accepts tablet and wafer food and enjoys a treat of freeze-dried bloodworm and tubifex. Its placid nature makes it ideal for the community aquarium. Maximum adult size: 23 cm (9 in).

### ◀ Kuhli loach

*Pangio kuhlii*

The kuhli loach from Southeast Asia is a long-standing aquarium favorite. Although the elongated body resembles that of an eel, it is a member of the carp family. The main reason for its appeal is its striking pattern of vivid orange-yellow spots or stripes on a matt black body. The kuhli loach is a notorious escapologist, so make sure your tank has a tight-fitting lid. Being nocturnal, it will hide during the brightest part of the day, emerging when aquarium light levels are reduced in the evening. Be sure to provide some hiding places so that this bottom-dwelling loach can take refuge during the day. It accepts crushed flake food and enjoys a treat of freeze-dried live foods, such as bloodworm and tubifex. Maximum adult size: 12 cm (4.7 in).

# RAINBOWFISH

Very few aquarium fish come from Australia, but rainbowfish are the exception. Many species are also found in the surrounding Southeast Asian region. As they become increasingly common in aquarium shops, their popularity is rising. This group of fish have a unique body shape and introduce a metallic color accent not found in many other aquarium fish. Other attractions include their placid nature and active lifestyle — both ideal traits in community fish. They are best kept in a small shoal to help them feel secure, and make a bold centerpiece in the display. In fact, an aquarium can easily be turned over to these fish, as they capture interest at the expense of other species. They will feed on tablet and wafer food, with treats of freeze-dried bloodworms and brineshrimp.

## Threadfin Rainbowfish ▼
### *Iriatherina werneri*
A unique display of fins give rise to this rainbowfish's common name. In the male, the double dorsal fin has two distinct shapes: the front fin is round and lobe-shaped, while the rear fin is tapered and threadlike. The rear dorsal fin is mirrored by an extended anal fin. Both are jet black and extend beyond the red-edged tail. These fin extensions are absent in the females. Being one of the smallest rainbowfish species, the threadfin is suited to any size of display. It occupies the middle and upper layers, where it needs access to dense plant cover. Do not keep it with Siamese fighters or boisterous barbs that will nip the males' extended fins. Maximum adult size: 5 cm (2 in).

## ▲ Red Rainbowfish
### *Glossolepis incisus*
Males of this midwater species have a strangely small head in relation to the huge body with a distinctive high back. Whereas males are a stunning red, females are more yellow and do not have the high back. Although it is an active fish it has a placid nature, which allows it to mix with all other community fish, making it the star of many displays. Provide some cover with dense planting and check your water chemistry before buying these fish; they prefer slightly alkaline water, with a reasonable level of hardness. If the water is soft, you should add some hardness minerals and salts. Do not keep it in small displays owing to its mature adult size. Maximum adult size: 15 cm (6 in).

*When displaying, these young males will raise the long dorsal fin like a flag.*

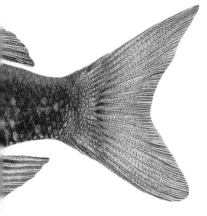

### ❧ Boesman's Rainbowfish

*Melanotaenia boesmani*

The stunning colors of Boesman's Rainbowfish from New Guinea have made it a firm favorite with many aquarium-keepers. In adult fish, the head and front half of the body are blue, in stark contrast to the rear half, which is a mixture of red and gold. Do not be deterred from buying the fish you see in aquarium shops; they will probably be juveniles with only a hint of the coloration that will develop with maturity. This peaceful, midwater fish appreciates the cover provided by dense planting, but is less sensitive than other rainbowfish are to water conditions. Nevertheless, be sure to maintain a stable pH above 7. Maximum adult size: 10 cm (4 in).

### ❧ *Melanotaenia praecox*

Metallic blue flanks and bright red dorsal, anal and caudal fins make this fish a real showstopper. Like other rainbowfish, it has a placid nature and enjoys the company of its own species. The flow from the power filter will provide a current in which this lively, midwater-swimming fish from Australia can play. Be sure to provide some plant cover. *M. praecox* prefers slightly acidic conditions, pH 6–7.5, and can tolerate reasonably soft water. Maximum adult size: 6 cm (2.4 in).

## ▲ Western Rainbowfish

*Melanotaenia splendida australis*

This vividly colored member of the rainbowfish family does best when housed in a larger display with four or five others of the same species. Like most rainbowfish it prefers plenty of open swimming space, but otherwise is one of the less demanding species. Feed them on a good-quality flake or granular food. Young specimens are a plain silver color and it may take up to a year for the full colors to develop, but the wait is worth it. The red and blue flanks are a great contrast to other rainbowfish. Maximum adult size: males 10 cm (4 in); females 8 cm (3.2 in).

## ▼ Banded Rainbowfish

*Melanotaenia trifasciata*

This multicolored member of the rainbowfish family makes a superb addition to a medium-sized display. The overall colors of the fish are subject to regional variation and range from gold green to silver blue. However, regardless of body color, all the fish have a black stripe that runs from head to tail, and red dorsal, anal and caudal fins. They are placid midwater swimmers that appreciate some dense plant cover. Maximum adult size: 12 cm (4.7 in).

# CHARACINS

### Headstander >

*Anostomus ternetzi*

Its unusual behavior makes the headstander an interesting subject for the aquarium. As its name implies, it often hangs head down in the water. Provide some hiding places and tall stem plants to help this placid midwater swimmer feel secure, and offer it a diet of flake food. Maximum adult size: 16 cm (6.2 in).

### Three-Lined Pencilfish ▼

*Nannostomus trifasciatus*

Pencilfish are a timid group that bring a sense of calm to the aquarium. Three-lined pencilfish have a wonderful set of markings based around three predominant horizontal stripes. Between the top two lines the body is gold, and at the base of each fin there is a scarlet red patch. Feed these midwater swimmers with flake food and provide them with some hiding places. Do not keep pencilfish with busy tankmates that will intimidate them. This midwater swimmer from Brazil will spend most of its time holding station amid the security of aquarium plants, making it easy to take a long look at this charming little fish. Maximum adult size: 10 cm (4 in).

## Marbled Hatchetfish ❯

*Carnegiella strigata strigata*

The marbled hatchetfish is the most common member of a group of fish that spend their time just below the water surface looking for food. The upturned jaw indicates that they are surface feeders, and although they accept flake foods, you should supplement their diet with frozen or freeze-dried bloodworm and daphnia. Provide some surface cover of floating plants. The body shape of these very streamlined fish from Peru resembles the keel of a yacht and gives them excellent stability in fast-moving water. They can often be seen holding position in the flow from the filter without apparently moving at all. They are able to jump and fly out of the water, so always provide a secure lid. Maximum adult size: 4 cm (1.6 in).

## ▼ One-Lined or Hockey Stick Pencilfish

*Nannobrycon unifasciatus*

This delicate species from Brazil is ideal for the smallest of quiet community displays, where it will swim in midwater at a head-up angle. It has an interesting pattern, namely a black stripe along each flank that extends into the lower lobe of the tail only. Like all pencilfish, it is timid and will only do well in a well-planted tank with plenty of hiding places. House pencilfish with placid tankmates, and always keep them in a shoal of at least five fish as they feel most at home when schooling. Offer a diet of flake food. Maximum adult size: 6 cm (2.4 in).

# KILLIFISH & ANABANTIDS

## Lyretail Killifish ▶
### Aphyosemion australe

Killifish belong to one of the more specialist groups of aquarium fish that are occasionally seen in mainstream aquarium shops. Most species require acidic water, which means they are not suitable for keeping with many other community species. *A. australe*, from West Africa, may be offered for sale in your aquarium shop, having been acclimatized to water above pH 7. If you do buy one, make sure your water chemistry at home is suitable. The pH level should be no higher than 7.5 and hardness up to 18°dH. If you can provide the right water conditions in a densely planted tank, the midwater-swimming killifish will reward you with stunning displays of vibrant colors and patterns, mostly displayed on a gold-toned body. Offer them a diet of flake food, plus freeze-dried bloodworms and brineshrimp. Maximum adult size: 6 cm (2.4 in).

## ▲ Siamese Fighting Fish
### Betta splendens

The common name of the Siamese fighting fish (an Anabantid) stems from the male's instinct to fight till the death if another male approaches. For this reason, you should never keep more than one male in the same tank. However, you can house females together, as they are relatively quiet. Never keep a female with a male as he will kill her if she is not ready to breed. Provide them with plant cover into which they can retreat to evade an amorous male if they are not ready to breed. The male's long flowing fins in shades of red, blue, green and gold make a wonderful showpiece in the aquarium. Never keep them with fin-nipping barbs, such as tiger barbs, to whom they represent an irresistible target. The fishes' water demands are usually easy to meet, as they will do well in all but the real extremes of fishkeeping pH values. Offer a diet of flake and freeze-dried bloodworms and daphnia, and provide plenty of surface plant cover, as this is where the male fighters like to prowl. Maximum adult size: 6–7 cm (2.4–2.75 in).

## Fish to avoid

The following species are commonly offered for sale in aquarium shops but are not suitable as community fish.

Plecostomus, or plec (*Hypostomus punctatus*) This fish simply grows too large and destructive for a community display. A juvenile offered for sale is a tempting prospect but once it becomes a 30 cm (12 in)-long monster it can destroy your display. Far more suitable suckermouth catfish are available (see page 172–173). Another species to avoid for the same reason is gibbiceps plec (*Pterygoplichthys gibbiceps*).

The clown loach (Botia macracantha) is attractive but grows too large for our tank. The orange-finned loach (*Botia modesta*) is often offered for sale as an alternative to the clown loach (*Botia macracantha*). However, it is much more aggressive toward other fish and will harass more sedentary species until they become ill. The same can also be said for *Botia lohachata* and *Botia helodes*.

Never buy any predatory fish, however tempting they may look. Take the advice of your retailer regarding compatibility.

# FEEDING FISH

Aquarium fish need a regular balanced diet if they are to thrive, and they depend totally on the fishkeeper to provide it.

In their natural habitat, many fish feed on live foods that form part of the natural food chain. Replicating this food chain is not a practical option, but good-quality, manufactured food will supply all the fishes' requirements. You can supplement this diet with safe "live" foods in freeze-dried or frozen form.

Feeding your fish is one of the most useful tools for monitoring their health. Use this time to check that they are all coming out to feed and are in good physical condition. Careful observation will allow you to ensure that every fish gets its fair share of food.

## Flakes and pellets

Generally speaking, the most practical food source for community fish is a proprietary flake or pellet food. Flakes are ideal for small to medium-sized fish, measuring up to 6 cm (2.4 in). Larger fish will do better on the more bulky, granular pellet food. The key to choosing any manufactured food is to look for a reliable brand that provides a complete food, including the following constituents.

## Dried foods

Dried foods can provide the staple diet for most fish. Flake foods are the most common form and widely available.

Choose the appropriate foods for your fish. These sinking granules will suit bottom-feeding species.

**Protein** Fish need protein for growth and cell repair. It is also broken down to provide energy when required. Ideally, the protein should be provided by fish and/or shrimp meal, as these sources are easily assimilated without causing the fish to produce excess waste. For tropical aquarium fish, protein should constitute 35%–50% of the dry weight of the food.

**Fat, or fatty acids** Young fish use up more energy than adults and require a slightly higher proportion of fat in their diet to meet their needs. They use protein exclusively for growth. For adult fish, the fat content of the diet should be no greater than 6%. Any excess will go to waste and result in an oil slick on the surface of the water.

**Vitamins** All animals, including fish, need vitamins, and a deficiency can cause a variety of problems. Vitamin A is essential for growth, and vitamin C for healthy skin. Poor skin condition is harmful for fish, as the mucus on the skin is a first line of defence against disease. Vitamin $B_3$ enables fish to process the protein in their food. Vitamin $D_3$ is essential for healthy bones; without it, fish may develop weak, deformed skeletons.

Commercial fish foods always contain a range of vitamins, but these are easily destroyed by age, air and moisture. Always keep fish food in a dry, cool place and use before the "Best Before" date.

**Carbohydrates** Generally, fish are better able to use fats and proteins, rather

*Left:* Flake foods are easy to use, but do not be tempted to overfeed. Offer a small amount at first; you can always add more later. In time, some fish may even take individual flakes from your fingers.

*Below:* Fish will soon respond to the arrival of food. This is a good opportunity to check that they are all present and feeding normally. Make sure that fish at all levels in the tank are getting food.

## Tablets and wafers

*Tablet foods are much like flake foods, but in a different form.*

*Algae wafers are ideal for herbivorous algae-eaters and bottom-feeding catfish.*

**Left:** *Tablets that are stuck onto the glass can be used to bring fish to the front of the tank for observation. As it disintegrates, the food attracts fish from all parts of the aquarium.*

than carbohydrates, for their energy needs. A food may be high in energy, but if most of this is supplied as carbohydrate, the fish may not be able to use it as well. Carbohydrates are vegetable in origin and include complex sugars such as starch, as well as cellulose (fiber). Artificial diets have a relatively reduced fiber content.

**Color enhancers** Certain ingredients harmlessly promote the natural skin colors of your aquarium fish, so that you see them at their best. Beta carotene and astaxanthin have long been used as effective color enhancers, but have been surpassed by the introduction of Spirulina. This freshwater algae has very high color enhancing properties and should be a standard ingredient in good-quality food.

**Immune system stimulants** This is a relatively new addition to aquarium fish foods. The immune system stimulant activates a fish's immune system so that it is ready to respond to any attack and does not need to wait for the attack itself to stimulate an immune response. This ensures that a fish is much more likely to fight off an infection successfully. The additive commonly used is beta glucan. An immune system stimulant should be a standard ingredient in fish food.

The right proportions of these ingredients are found in both flake and granular pellet foods. When buying new fish, it is always worth asking the retailer what type of food they have been accustomed to so that you can continue the same feeding regime in your home aquarium. Make any changes to the diet gradually.

## Tablet foods

Tablet foods are usually made from standard flake food pressed into a tablet form. They have been developed to make it easier to watch the fish while they feed. Push the tablet firmly onto the inside of the front glass, where the water and the pecking action of the fish will cause it to break up slowly. The main benefit from this feeding method is that all the food is in one place and the fish must come to it to feed, which most species will readily do. Only offer tablets as an alternative to other foods; the fish will ignore one of the foods and much of it will rot in the water.

## Wafers

A few species of fish, especially catfish and loaches, appreciate a high percentage of algae in their diet. Sinking wafers make it easier to supply the requirements of these bottom-dwelling fish. The hard wafers sink to the base of the aquarium, where they soften, so that the loaches and catfish can browse on them. It is a good idea to offer several smaller wafers, as some catfish can be quarrelsome over food and a timid individual may suffer if not given ample opportunity to feed.

## Freeze-dried foods

Some live foods, such as tubifex worms, naturally grow in stagnant water and can harbor disease organisms that you can unwittingly introduce to your fish. Freeze-dried foods are a safe alternative. They are irradiated with gamma rays that sterilize them, and then freeze dried to maintain the nutrient content and give them a long shelf life. While fish enjoy them, they are not nutritionally complete and are best offered as a treat in conjunction with the usual diet. Often, the foods are molded

into cubes that can be pressed onto the aquarium wall, where you can enjoy the resulting feeding frenzy and ensure that the block does not get washed under a plant or rock to rot.

## Frozen food

Frozen foods are also gamma-irradiated to remove pathogens, and then packed into blister packs prior to freezing. Keep them frozen until they are required, but allow them to thaw before feeding them to your fish. Placing the required amount in a little warm water in a shallow dish will speed up the process. The only drawback of this food is keeping it frozen; this usually means storing it with food for human consumption, which some family members might object to. Once the food

has thawed never refreeze it. Either use it immediately or throw it away.

## Live foods

As we have seen, some live foods can introduce diseases. However, most aquatic retailers are very careful to stock only live foods that have been specifically grown to feed fish and are very unlikely to harbor any pathogens. To be extra safe, buy saltwater creatures such as brineshrimp *(Artemia)* or copepods. There are no pathogens that can cross between saltwater and fresh, so these live foods are completely safe. They will not be able to live for long in freshwater, so only add as many as your fish can eat in a couple of minutes; however, the fish will consume them with such gusto that this should not

## Freeze-dried food

*Freeze-dried mosquito larvae can form part of a more varied diet.*

*Freeze-dried tubifex is a safe way of offering this invertebrate food.*

## Frozen food

*A defrosted cube of bloodworm makes a treat.*

## Vacation feeding

Aquarists are often concerned about how to feed their fish when they go away. There are various options. Healthy adult fish will happily go without food for a week or so. If you are away for longer than that, package up daily rations of flake or freeze-dried food in a twist of foil and leave them in the fridge for a friend or neighbor to administer. (Hide the tub of flake in case your helper is tempted to give the fish a bit extra.) Alternatively, invest in an autofeeder — a timer-controlled reservoir for flake or small granules — and program it to dispense one or more meals daily. Vacation feeding blocks are another option.

**Left:** *Vacation feeding blocks contain food in a type of chalky block that gradually dissolves, allowing the fish to eat the feed it contains. Small sticks release the food over a weekend. Larger blocks last for a week or more.*

**Right:** *This battery-operated autofeeder can dispense flakes or granules at preset times. The food compartment rotates and the contents drop into the tank. The amount of food released can be regulated and a one-touch feed button dispenses food on demand. Simply clamp onto the side of the aquarium.*

**Right:** *Daphnia, or water fleas, are microscopic creatures that make a good first food for newly hatched fry, as well as small fish. They are sometimes available in aquatic outlets.*

**Below:** *Suitable aquatic live foods include daphnia (left), bloodworms (center) and brineshrimp (right). They are sold in plastic bags full of water. Strain the contents through a fine net. Do not put the water into the aquarium.*

**Left:** *Bloodworms are midge larvae and fish relish them as part of their diet. As well as frozen, they are available in freeze-dried form from aquatic stores.*

**Right:** *Adding a batch of bloodworm to the aquarium prompts an immediate feeding response from your aquarium fish. You can watch the fish feed at close quarters as they devour the larvae.*

be a problem! An alternative is terrestrial foods such as earthworms, which make a suitable treat (particularly larger fish) if offered occasionally.

## How much should I feed?

Overfeeding is the most common cause of water quality problems, which in turn leads to fish health issues. It is therefore vital to gauge how much food you feed your fish. The golden rule is to try to feed as much food as your fish will consume in one minute, with no food left over or sinking to the bottom. With the exception of sinking tablets and wafers for bottom feeders, any food that reaches the bottom of the tank before it is eaten is a clear sign that too much food has been fed. Uneaten food will decompose in the aquarium, causing a release of toxic ammonia into the water as it rots.

## When should I feed the fish?

As feeding the fish is one of the few occasions when you can interact with them, choose a time when you can sit down and enjoy watching them. Fish can become accustomed to a set feeding time, so choose a time that suits you. Feed them once a day for the first two months after setting up the aquarium. This will allow the biological system to establish without placing an excessive strain on the filtration bacteria. Thereafter, you can feed the fish twice daily. Always make sure that no one else in the household has fed them first. This will avoid the risk of uneaten food being left to rot in the aquarium.

**Over the next four weeks the aquarium will continue to flourish and become the stunning display you planned.** ▶

# THE FINISHED DISPLAY

After twelve weeks, the aquarium is continuing to progress. Most things have turned out well, but the most difficult plants to grow — the *Hemianthus* and the *Glossostigma* in the foreground — are encountering some teething problems. They have not flourished as well as they should have. This could be the result of a number of factors: not enough light, not enough food, etc. The light issue can be resolved by adding a reflector to the front lamp in the aquarium. This will bounce all the light given out by the lamp down into the aquarium and increase the light intensity at the front, which should encourage the plants to put on more growth. If in time the plants show no signs of recovery, replace them before they rot in the aquarium, as we have done here.

The *Echinodorus cordifolius* is also showing less evidence of growth than before. This is because new plants will have been grown as an emergent plant, with leaves above water. Once the plant is completely submerged, it must produce submerged leaves as the emergent ones die away. Remove the emergent leaves, allowing room for the new submerged leaves to fill the space. This may take a few weeks. The continued $CO_2$ dosing and liquid feeding will create the correct conditions for the plants to thrive.

The biological filter has matured, with no signs of any ammonia and nitrite. Nitrate is being kept under control by regular water changes and the fish are proving the real stars of the show. Tablet food stuck to the inside of the glass encourages them to congregate in the central part of the aquarium, creating a dynamic kaleidoscope of color in the heart of the display.

This is how the display aquarium looks with a fresh planting of
Hemianthus and Glossostigma in the foreground area.

# THIS IS JUST THE BEGINNING

The completed aquarium will now be the main attraction in the room chosen for it. In the twelve weeks of development, from selecting the rocks, wood and plants through to adding the fish, a bare glass tank has been transformed into a unique display to be proud of. With the wide range of decor, plants and fish available to hobbyists today, it is possible to create an almost endless variety of "designs" in a home aquarium. One avenue to explore is to recreate natural environments from around the world, such as an Amazon pool, an African stream, a Southeast Asian swamp or a brackish estuary.

With proper care, the display will provide pleasure every day for years to come. It will be constantly changing, however, as plants grow larger or lose leaves before growing new ones. Some plants may flower or produce daughter plantlets on runners, and these will be ideal raw material for propagating new plants, as explained on page 199.

**Below:** *The fish will explore most areas of the aquarium, some enjoying the flow from the pumps, while others will avoid it. As the plants grow, they will sway in the water flow from the filter, adding more movement to the display.*

**Below:** *The male and female cockatoo cichlids have taken center stage and will play out their courtship roles amongst the rocks and bogwood. Their breeding rituals add a new dimension to the display.*

**Right:** *The three "windows" present different viewing angles into the display, allowing us to follow the fish as they swim between the plants. An aquarium is literally a living picture that will quickly become everyone's focus of attention.*

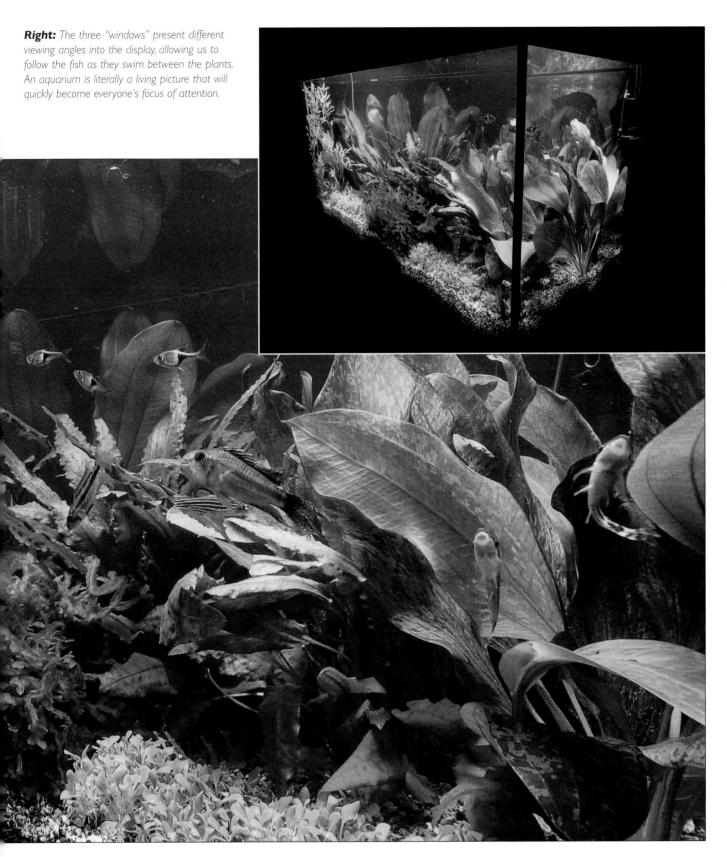

# POTENTIAL HEALTH ISSUES

To ensure that the fish stay healthy in our display aquarium, it is vital to carry out routine maintenance as described on pages 194–199. Should the water quality start to decline through lack of maintenance then we run the risk of fish succumbing to diseases that their immune system normally keeps at bay. Should this happen, we must be able to diagnose what our fish are suffering from and provide the appropriate treatment. The "unfortunate" fish featured here has symptoms of all the common ailments that tropical freshwater fish may suffer from in the aquarium. Most are easily identifiable and can be cured using proprietary treatments. The key approach to monitoring the health of your fish is to be observant. Watching your fish as you feed them every day is the ideal opportunity to check their "body language." An unwell fish will not feed as well as usual or not at all and may swim around with clamped fins held tight to the body. Look closely at any fish behaving unnaturally for symptoms that match those shown here. This will help you identify the problem and apply the best remedy.

### Slime patches

*These are caused by the fish's immune response to protozoan skin parasites. In severe cases, the slime (mucus) patches will cover most of the body. May be accompanied by flicking behavior and clamped, folded fins. Use an antiparasite treatment.*

### Mouth rot

*Cottonwool-like growths around the mouth could be a bacterial or fungal infection. Use a treatment that will tackle both types of infection.*

### Swollen eyes

*These may be caused by an internal bacterial infection and can be seen in fish affected by dropsy. A tumour behind the eye could also cause this symptom.*

### Rapid gill movements

*These could be caused by high nitrite levels or other water quality problems, as well as parasites or bacterial infection. Check the water quality and make a change if necessary. Otherwise treat with a suitable medication.*

### White spots

*White spots like sugar grains on the skin and gills are signs of a parasite infection called white spot, one of the most commonly seen problems among aquarium fish. Treatments target the free-swimming stages of the parasite's life cycle and to be effective must be carried out over a period of a few days. Left untreated, white spots will quickly spread to all the fish in the aquarium.*

## Fine gold spots

*Very fine gold spots are typical symptoms of velvet disease caused by a skin parasite. Treat quickly with a targeted antiparasite remedy.*

## Fungus

*Any skin damage may become infected with fungus to produce cottonwool-like growths. To be sure, use a medication that will deal with both external bacteria and fungus.*

## Ragged fins

*Ragged edges to the fins, which may also be red and sore, are signs of a bacterial infection known as finrot. Use an antibacterial treatment to stop it spreading to the body. Damaged fin tissue may regrow once the infection has been cured.*

## Using medications

**1** Carefully measure out the correct amount of treatment or the number of drops recommended and add this to a jug of water taken from the aquarium.

**2** Mix the treatment into the water in the jug. Make sure that the spoon or other implement you use to mix the treatment is clean and free from any chemicals or other contamination.

**3** Slowly pour the treatment over the surface of the aquarium. Diluting the mixture in this way will ensure an even distribution of the medication.

## Important notes

Check that any treatment you buy is easy to use and has clear instructions on how to use any pipettes or measuring cups included.

Keep a note of the volume of your aquarium (see page 38) as this will allow you to dose accurately. Overdosing will probably be lethal to all your fish!

Always keep fish medication locked up out of the reach of children. Most treatments for aquarium use contain potentially harmful chemicals.

## Protruding scales

*Swelling with scales protruding like a pinecone, commonly known as dropsy, is caused by an internal bacterial infection that inhibits the fish's ability to control the level of water in its body. Use an internal bacterial treatment.*

**Right:** *A Cuming's barb with classic signs of dropsy. The whole body is swollen, making the head appear relatively small. The eyes are protruding. Difficult to treat, but if diagnosed early it can be cured with proprietary treatments.*

## A LIVING DISPLAY

The display aquarium you have created is a living environment that will change and develop over a period of time. To keep it looking good, it is vital to carry out routine maintenance. All the living organisms in the aquarium produce waste. If this is allowed to build up, the biological cycles will become overloaded and the display will disintegrate. Routine maintenance tasks are presented here in easy-to-follow time slots. By following this regime you will be able to keep your display looking as stunning as it did when you added your last batch of fish.

### Essential supplies

As well as making sure you have good supplies of fish food and plant fertilizers, it is vital to have the following supplies and spare parts:

Heaterstat
Suckers
Bearings, impeller and O-ring
  seals for filters
Filter wool and or foam
Other filter media being used
  in the system
Clean plastic bucket/bowl
Activated carbon
Thermometer
Nets
Fuses
Fluorescent tubes
Starters for fluorescent tubes
Airline and airstones
Test kits
Tap water conditioner
Filter start-up product

## EVERY DAY

Checking your aquarium every day should be a pleasure, not a chore. As a general rule, the more often a task is needed, the less time it takes. Most of the daily tasks take only a few minutes.

Check the water temperature.

Check for missing fish. Dead fish left undiscovered in the aquarium will pollute the water and threaten the well-being of the other inhabitants. Also check for signs of ill-health or distress, such as red marks on the body and gills, excess mucus, gasping at the surface or any other unusual behavior.

Check that the internal filter is working properly.

Feed the fish, making sure that they all receive some.

Check that the lights are working.

Remove any uneaten food that the fish do not seem interested in.

# EVERY 7–14 DAYS

Among the routine maintenance tasks that you need to carry out every 7–14 days, the most important ones are geared toward keeping the water in good condition, such as regular water changes and tests for toxic waste products.

Test the water for pH, ammonia, nitrite and nitrate levels.

▼

▲

Gently disturb any fine-leaved plants to remove trapped detritus.

▲

Clean the substrate with a gravel cleaner that will siphon off debris.

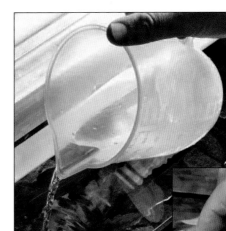

◀ Make a 15% water change and refill the aquarium with conditioned water at the same temperature.

◀ Clean the front and side glass of the aquarium to prevent a buildup of algae that can be very hard to remove later on.

Feed plants with liquid fertilizer. Follow the maker's instructions for the correct dosing levels. ▶

◀ Where fitted, clean the condensation cover to avoid a reduction in light to plants.

▲
◀ Remove dead or dying leaves.

# ROUTINE MAINTENANCE

## EVERY 4–6 WEEKS

The maintenance tasks necessary every 4–6 weeks center on the filter. This is the vital life-support system for the aquarium and needs regular attention to ensure that it is functioning properly. Any cleaning must be carried out with tank water to avoid disrupting the beneficial bacteria in the biological medium.

◀ Clean the internal filter, including the impeller and casing.

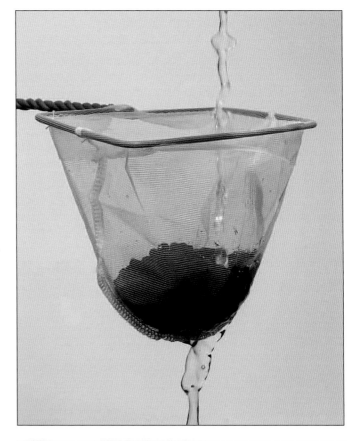

▶ If included, replace the activated carbon in the filter. Rinse it before use.

◀ Clean the filter foam in tank water.

▶ Renew the yeast-sugar solution in the $CO_2$ fertilization system and clean the inlet of the water pump.

▲ Clean any external filter media in tank water.

▲ Replace expendable filter media, such as filter wool.

## Every 6–12 months

The routine maintenance at this level focuses on replacing consumable pieces of aquarium equipment. Fluorescent tubes and parts of the filtration system do wear out, so to maintain optimum performance check and replace them before they fail completely.

Replace half the filter foam in the internal filter. Allow one month before replacing the other half. ▶

▲ Replace fluorescent tubes, even if they are still working.

Replace the filter pump impeller. ▶

## As needed

If the aquarium has a full display of plants, keeping these healthy and growing well is one of the long-term objectives of routine maintenance. And if they outgrow their space, they will need trimming back. Always be prepared for emergencies and make sure you have spares of essential items in stock.

◀ Replenish any tablet fertilizers for aquarium plants.

Trim tall plants to prevent them blocking light to other plants. Use trimmings for propagation. ▶

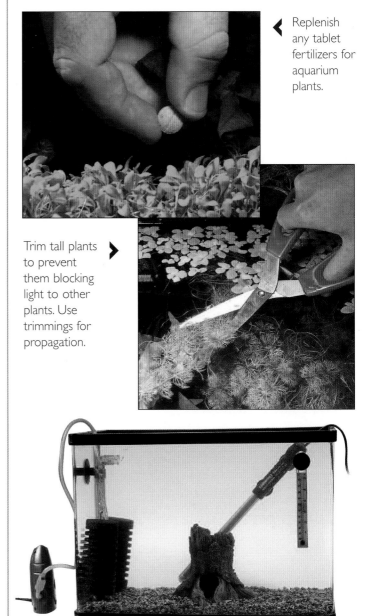

▲ Check the quarantine/hospital tank and make sure the filter is working properly in case the tank is needed for new fish or to treat existing stock with health remedies.

## UNDERSTANDING ALGAE

Algae are simple plants that grow in the aquatic environment. They are usually out-competed for food and light by the more advanced plants in the aquarium. However, if they do appear you should take quick action to remove them before they ruin your display. Algae can grow very quickly, so swift action is vital. Always ensure that any algae treatment you use is plant friendly, as some may kill your plants as well as the algae. Various types of algae may develop in the aquarium.

**Green water algae** will turn your aquarium into "pea soup" as the algae bloom in the presence of too much light and nutrients. You can cut down excess light by altering your lighting timer or ensuring that no direct sunlight falls across the tank. Use a flocculent algae remover to remedy the problem.

**Hair algae** will grow like string from any internal surface in the aquarium, including the plants. The strands are usually green but can also be black or brown. Try and remove as much as possible by hand before adding a suitable treatment. Experiment by shortening the aquarium

lighting time to achieve a period that does not encourage the algae growth. Also increase the $CO_2$ concentration.

**Slime algae** appear to be similar to fine-hair algae, but they are species of bacteria. This green/brown carpet of slime can engulf an aquarium in a matter of a few days. It takes a hold only when

*Right:* A glistening shroud of blue-green slime algae spreads rapidly over the fronds of an aquatic fern.

water quality is poor and when essential maintenance to reduce organic waste, such as removing uneaten food and dead leaves and gravel cleaning, has been missed. The best remedy is to carry out a water change, add a sludge control antibacterial product to the aquarium and return to the regular maintenance regime. It will often die back as quickly as it appeared.

*Left:* Green water is a suspension of single algae cells that multiply rapidly in nutrient-rich, illuminated water.

*Below:* Neglected maintenance has allowed brown strands of hair algae to suffocate the plants they cover.

## The color of water

Crystal-clear water may not necessarily be healthy, since it may contain toxic levels of ammonia and/or nitrite that represent invisible dangers to the livestock in your aquarium. However, there are some more tangible signs in the color and condition of the tank water that can point to the following possible causes:

Yellow-stained water is old. Missing water changes causes a build-up of organic dyes. The remedy is to make an immediate 20% water change, followed by a return to regular 15% water changes. Also add or change the activated carbon in the filter.

Brown tea-colored water is usually caused by tannic acids leaching from bogwood that has not been soaked for long enough. If possible, remove the wood and soak it as recommended on page 30. Alternatively, increase the frequency of partial water changes. Some chemical filtration products will remove these dyes.

Brown / green / gray cloudy water is usually caused by overfeeding and lack of aquarium maintenance. Carry out a water change and clean the filter. Use a proprietary flocculent treatment to stick the particles together so they can be removed by the filter.

*Above:* Tannins released from the bogwood have turned this water tea brown. Not usually a threat to fish health, but unsightly.

## Propagating from cuttings

Trimming plants to tidy up the tank can provide raw material for propagation. Most stem plants can be propagated by cuttings taken from both the top and middle stem areas. Taking cuttings is also a way of "thickening" up plants by stimulating side shoots.

**1** To take a top cutting, snip off a length of stem with several leaves or nodes. Cut between the nodes with sharp scissors. For the best results, take cuttings from the fastest growing and/or healthiest stem.

**2** Strip away the leaves from one or two nodes at the base of the cutting to allow the plant to root more quickly. Roots will form from the stripped node. Make sure it is beneath the substrate when planting.

**3** Push the cutting into the substrate so that the lower leaves are just resting on the substrate surface. Roots should grow from the base and the plant will establish quickly, although lower leaves may die off.

## Propagating from a runner

Many plants produce several daughter plants from one runner, so to obtain a larger number of plants, do not remove the runner until it has produced at least five or six plants.

The mother plant may produce more than one runner at a time.

These daughter plants of Echinodorus sp. are ready to be planted in the substrate.

**2** Separate the individual plants, or "slips," leaving a small length of runner on either side. Handle them carefully, holding them by the leaf and not by the stem.

**1** Once the "mother" plant has produced a number of daughter plants with at least two or three leaves each, you can cut the runner with a pair of sharp scissors.

**3** Put each new plant into the substrate, leaving a gap of at least 5 cm (2 in) between the plants to allow for future growth.

# INDEX

# FISH INDEX

# FISH INDEX

# Plant index

# CREDITS

## Credits

The publishers would like to thank the following photographers for providing images, credited here by page number and position: (B) Bottom, (T) Top, (C) Center, (BL) Bottom left, etc.

Aqua Press (M-P & C Piednoir): 11(B), 12(T), 58(L), 60(T), 62–63(BC), 63(R), 64(TR), 71(BR), 73(TC), 74–75(BC), 77(R), 78–79(C), 113(TL), 122(T,B), 123(B), 124(T,B), 124–125(B), 125(B), 126–127(B), 128(B), 130(C), 131(B), 132(B), 133(T), 134(B), 134–135(T), 135(T), 137(T,B), 138(CL,BR), 139(C), 162(C), 162–163(B), 164(B), 164–165(T), 166–167(B), 167(T), 168(T,B), 170–171(B), 172–173(C), 173, 176(L,T,C,B) 179(B), 180(B), 181(T), 182(B)

Peter Hiscock 147

Jan-Eric Larsson-Rubenowitz 141(T)

Photomax (Max Gibbs): 172(T)

William A Tomey: 170(T,C), 176(T)

Tropica (Ole Pedersen): 84(T)

## Acknowledgments

The publishers would like to thank: Simon Williams at J & K Aquatics, Taunton, Somerset for supplying the fish featured in the display aquarium; Martin Pedersen of Tropica Aquarium Plants, A/S, Hjortshøj, Denmark, for supplying plants for photography; Kevin Chambers of Arcadia for supplying lighting equipment for photography; Keith Cocker of the Norwich Aquarist Society for help with fish photography; David Cummings of Kesgrave Tropicals for supplying aquarium equipment; Swallow Aquatics, Rayleigh, Essex for providing fish and onsite photographic facilities. Also Maidenhead Aquatics, Crowland and Maidenhead Aquatics, Woodbridge, for their generous help.

Index compiled by Amanda O'Neill.

## Publisher's note

The information and recommendations in this book are given without guarantee on the part of the author and publishers, who disclaim any liability with the use of this material.